El Método de Aprendizaje *South Beach* para inglés conversacional

Por Erasmus Cromwell- Smith

El método de aprendizaje South Beach para inglés conversacional
© Erasmus Cromwell-Smith
© RCHC LLC

All rights reserved. No part of this book or any portion may be reproduced or used in any form or by any electronic or mechanical means, without the express written permission from the copyrighted owner, except for the use of brief quotations in a book review.

ISBN: 1-11457789061

Publisher: Erasmus Press
Editor and Proofreading: Elisa Arraiz Lucca
Cover Design and Interior Design: Abjini Shamanik
www.erasmuscromwellsmith.com

Este curso es radicalmente distinto a ningún otro en el sentido de que usted revisitará la gramática del español a los efectos de refrescar ciertas reglas y prácticas de nuestro lenguaje.

Como verá, hay muchas cosas que decimos de cierta manera, simplemente por costumbre, sin saber si están bien dichas o no, sin ni siquiera saber por qué hablamos así.

El supuesto es sencillo, regresamos y revisitamos nuestro lenguaje a los efectos de aprender ciertos conceptos para poder traducir de manera exacta el inglés, en otras palabras, la manera como construimos las frases con las que hablamos nuestro idioma tienen que ser gramaticalmente correctas para que también podamos traducir al inglés correctamente, porque si nuestra oración en español es gramaticalmente incorrecta, la traducción de la misma al inglés también lo será.

INGLÉS CONVERSACIONAL

- Este curso le permitirá aprender inglés con solo unas pocas horas de estudio.
- Este curso desvirtúa completamente la creencia acerca de que el inglés es un idioma muy difícil de aprender.
- De hecho, ambos idiomas se hablan de la misma manera (casi como una imagen en un espejo).
- La fundación de este programa son <u>Los Verbos Infinitivos.</u>
- Usted aprenderá a hablar inglés a través de cuatro formatos en fórmula que simplifican significativamente el cómo hablar inglés.Todos ellos basados en <u>Los Verbos Infinitivos.</u>
- Este curso también enseña cómo pronunciar correctamente las palabras en inglés.
- Así mismo, permite estudiar y aprender la mayoría de los verbos en inglés,únicamente en el tiempo infinitivo, prácticamente sin aprender las conjugaciones, las cuales toman muchísimas horas de aprendizaje.
- En este curso se estudian los cuatro verbos "gatillo" y sus conjugaciones. Estos verbos, una vez aprendidos, permiten establecer prácticamente cualquier tipo de conversación.

El método de aprendizaje South Beach para inglés conversacional

Los 14 Pasos de aprendizaje

1er.	PASO	LAS VOCALES	(LECCIÓN No. 1)	9
2do.	PASO	EL ALFABETO	(LECCIÓN No. 1)	11
3er.	PASO	LOS PRONOMBRES	(LECCIÓN No. 2)	15
4to.	PASO	LAS PALABRAS MÁGICAS	(LECCIÓN No. 3)	21
5to.	PASO	POSESIVO Y REFLEXIVO	(LECCIÓN No. 3)	30
6to.	PASO	VERBOS INFINITIVOS	(LECCIÓN No. 4)	32
7mo.	PASO	LOS 4 VERBOS GATILLO	(LECCIONES No. 5, 6, 7, 8 Y 9)	40
8vo.	PASO	LOS 4 FORMATOS	(LECCIONES No. 10, 11, 12 Y 13)	57
9no.	PASO	LOS 11 VERBOS	(LECCIÓN No. 14)	71
10mo.	PASO	PREGUNTAS/NEGACIONES	(LECCIÓN No. 15)	73
11vo.	PASO	HAY/HUBO/HABRÁ	(LECCIÓN No. 16)	75
12vo.	PASO	ER – EST Y "Y"	(LECCIÓN No. 17)	77
13vo.	PASO	EL VERBO TO HAVE	(LECCIÓN No. 18)	80
14vo.	PASO	ACABO DE	(LECCIÓN No. 19)	82

El método de aprendizaje South Beach para inglés conversacional

El Inglés

Es muy

Fácil

De aprender e igualmente

Fácil de hablar

El método de aprendizaje South Beach para inglés conversacional

EMPECEMOS

En gran parte:

El inglés se habla de la misma manera como se habla el español.

La mayoría de las reglas gramaticales (incluyendo sus nombres) son las mismas.

Las frases son estructuradas de la misma manera. Adicionalmente, muchas palabras son muy similares pero pronunciadas de manera diferente.

Entonces, ¡desmontemos juntos la idea de que el inglés es un idioma difícil de aprender!

1er. Paso de Aprendizaje

Todo comienza con

las 5 vocales

¡Aprenda a pronunciarlas correctamente!

Lección No. 1: Part E 1

LO BÁSICO PRIMERO

Vocal en inglés	Pronunciación en inglés Fácil: La pronunciación está entre paréntesis ( )				
A (Ei)	Lea en voz alta Ei	otra vez Ei	otra vez Ei	otra vez Ei	Ei
E (i)	i	i	i	i	i
I (Ai)	Ai	Ai	Ai	Ai	Ai
O (Ou)	Ou	Ou	Ou	Ou	Ou
U (iU)	iU	iU	iU	iU	iU

Ahora practiquemos juntos en voz alta: **Ei-i-Ai-Ou-iU**

Ahora hágalo más rápido: **Ei-i-Ai-Ou-iU** aún más rápido: **Ei-i-Ai-Ou-iU**

Siga practicando: **Ei-i-Ai-Ou-iU** Hasta que lo memorice.

Ei-i-Ai-Ou-iU Repita y memorice los sonidos.

A-E-I-O-U Trate de hacerlo más y más rápido.

2do. Paso de Aprendizaje

Lo siguiente es aprender

El Alfabeto

¡En (paréntesis) encontrará la pronunciación en español!

El método de aprendizaje South Beach para inglés conversacional

LeCCIÓn No. 1 : Part E 2

Pronunciación y fonética del Alfabeto en inglés

A (ei)	B (bi)	C (si)	D (di)	E (i)	F (ef)
G (yi)	H (eich)	I (ai)	J (yei)	K(kei)	L (el)
M (em)	N (en)	O (ou)	P (pi)	Q (kiu)	R (ar)
S (es)	T (ti)	U (iu)	V (vi)	W (doble- iu)	
X (ex)	Y (uai)	Z (zzi)			

El método de aprendizaje South Beach para inglés conversacional

2do. Paso de Aprendizaje

También es muy útil
Aprender

¡Los Números!

LeCCIÓn No. 1 : Part E 3

Uno One	Dos Two	Tres Three	Cuatro Four	Cinco Five	Seis Six	Siete Seven	Ocho Eight	Nueve Nine
Diez Ten	Veinte Twenty	Treinta Thirty	Cuarenta Forty	Cincuenta Fifty	Sesenta Sixty	Setenta Seventy	Ochenta Eighty	Noventa Ninety

Cien One hundred	Doscientos Two hundred	Trescientos Three hundred	Cuatrocientos Four hundred
Quinientos Five hundred	Seiscientos Six hundred	Setecientos Seven hundred	Ochocientos Eight hundred
Novecientos Nine hundred	Mil One thousand	Diez mil Ten thousand	Cien mil One hundred thousand
Un millón One million	Cien millones One hundred million	Mil millones/Un millardo One billion	Un trillón One trillion

El método de aprendizaje South Beach para inglés conversacional

3er. Paso de Aprendizaje

Una vez aprendidos el alfabeto y las vocales,
el próximo paso es aprender:

Los Pronombres

LeCCIÓn No. 2 : Part E 1

(Yo-Usted)	() ¡Fácll Solo Léalo!
Léalo en voz alta I (ai) - Yo	Léalo en voz alta You (yu) –Usted
Léalo en voz alta I (ai) - Yo	Léalo en voz alta You (yu) –Usted
Léalo en voz alta I (ai) - Yo	Léalo en voz alta You (yu) –Usted
Léalo en voz alta I (ai) - Yo	Léalo en voz alta You (yu) –Usted
Léalo en voz alta I (ai) - Yo	Léalo en voz alta You (yu) –Usted
Léalo en voz alta I (ai) - Yo	Léalo en voz alta You (yu) –Usted
Léalo en voz alta I (ai) - Yo	Léalo en voz alta You (yu) –Usted
Léalo en voz alta I (ai) - Yo	Léalo en voz alta You (yu) –Usted
(En Inglés) Recuerde, I (ai) es Yo	(En Inglés) You (yu) es Usted

El método de aprendizaje South Beach para inglés conversacional

LeCCIÓn No. 2 : Part E 2

(El-Ella)	() ¡Fácil Solo Léalo!
Léalo en voz alta **He (ji) - El**	Léalo en voz alta **She (shi) – Ella**
Léalo en voz alta **He (ji) - El**	Léalo en voz alta **She (shi) – Ella**
Léalo en voz alta **He (ji) - El**	Léalo en voz alta **She (shi) – Ella**
Léalo en voz alta **He (ji) - El**	Léalo en voz alta **She (shi) – Ella**
Léalo en voz alta **He (ji) - El**	Léalo en voz alta **She (shi) – Ella**
Léalo en voz alta **He (ji) - El**	Léalo en voz alta **She (shi) – Ella**
Léalo en voz alta **He (ji) - El**	Léalo en voz alta **She (shi) – Ella**
Léalo en voz alta **He (ji) - El**	Léalo en voz alta **She (shi) – Ella**
(En Inglés) Recuerde, <u>He</u> (ji) es <u>El</u>	(En Inglés) <u>She</u> (shi) es <u>Ella</u>

El método de aprendizaje South Beach para inglés conversacional

LeCCIÓn No. 2 : Part E 3

(Nosotros-Ustedes)	() ¡Fácil Solo Léalo!
Léalo en voz alta We (gui) - Nosotros	Léalo en voz alta You (yu) –Ustedes
Léalo en voz alta We (gui) - Nosotros	Léalo en voz alta You (yu) –Ustedes
Léalo en voz alta We (gui) - Nosotros	Léalo en voz alta You (yu) –Ustedes
Léalo en voz alta We (gui) - Nosotros	Léalo en voz alta You (yu) –Ustedes
Léalo en voz alta We (gui) - Nosotros	Léalo en voz alta You (yu) –Ustedes
Léalo en voz alta We (gui) - Nosotros	Léalo en voz alta You (yu) –Ustedes
Léalo en voz alta We (gui) - Nosotros	Léalo en voz alta You (yu) –Ustedes
Léalo en voz alta We (gui) - Nosotros	Léalo en voz alta You (yu) –Ustedes
(En Inglés) Recuerde, We (gui) es Nosotros	(En Inglés) You (yu) es Ustedes

El método de aprendizaje South Beach para inglés conversacional

LeCCIÓn No. 2 : Part E 4

(Ellos, Eso/Esto)	() ¡Fácil Solo Léalo!
Léalo en voz alta **They (dei) - Ellos**	Léalo en voz alta **It (it) Eso/Esto**
Léalo en voz alta **They (dei) - Ellos**	Léalo en voz alta **It (it) Eso/Esto**
Léalo en voz alta **They (dei) - Ellos**	Léalo en voz alta **It (it) Eso/Esto**
Léalo en voz alta **They (dei) - Ellos**	Léalo en voz alta **It (it) Eso/Esto**
Léalo en voz alta **They (dei) - Ellos**	Léalo en voz alta **It (it) Eso/Esto**
Léalo en voz alta **They (dei) - Ellos**	Léalo en voz alta **It (it) Eso/Esto**
Léalo en voz alta **They (dei) - Ellos**	Léalo en voz alta **It (it) Eso/Esto**
Léalo en voz alta **They (dei) - Ellos**	Léalo en voz alta **It (it) Eso/Esto**
(En Inglés) **Recuerde, They (dei) es Ellos**	(En Inglés) **It (it) es Eso/Esto**

El método de aprendizaje South Beach para inglés conversacional

LeCCIÓn No. 2 : Part E 5

Sumario	Pronombres	() ¡Fácil Solo Léalo!
Continuemos Practicando	I (ai) - Yo	Lea los (paréntesis) Pronúncielo 5 veces
	You (yu) - Usted	Este también 5 veces
	He (ji) - El	Este también 5 veces
	She (shi) - Ella	Continúe 5 veces también
	We (gui) - Nosotros	Pronúncielo 5 veces
	You (yu) - Ustedes	Este también 5 veces
	They (dei) - Ellos	Continúe 5 veces también
	It (it) - Eso/ Esto	Este también 5 veces

El método de aprendizaje South Beach para inglés conversacional

4to. Paso de Aprendizaje

Las siguientes

Palabras Mágicas

Son esenciales en cualquier conversación

¡PRACTÍQUELAS!

LeCCIÓn No. 3 : Part E 1

Introduzcamos 10 palabras que son esenciales en cualquier conversación

An/A	=	un uno / una unos / unas	Yes (yes) = Si No (nou) = No
The (de)	=	El La Los Las	At (at) = En el (lugar) En los (lugares) A las (horas)
And (and)	=	Y	To (to) = A
With (guid)	=	Con	That (Dat) = Eso (señalar) Que (enfatizar)
Or (or)	=	O	This (Dis) = Esto

El método de aprendizaje South Beach para inglés conversacional

LeCCIÓn No. 3 : Part E 2

What (Guat)	=	Cuál, Qué	But (bot)	=	Pero
When (Guen)	=	Cuándo	Whose (jus)	=	De quién
Where (Guere)	=	Dónde	Who (ju)	=	Quién
Why (Guai)	=	Porqué	Which (guich)	=	Cuál
Whether (Gueder)	=	Bien sea, O	How (jau)	=	Cómo
To (to)	=	A	For (for)	=	Por, para
From (from)	=	De, Desde	While (guail)	=	Mientras
How Many (jau meny)	=	Cuántos	Whom (jum)	=	Con quién
For (for)	=	Para, por	As	=	Tal como
More than	=	Más que	How Much (jau moch)	=	Cuánto cuesta

El método de aprendizaje South Beach para inglés conversacional

LeCCIÓn No. 3 : Part E 2

A: To
Adentro: Inside
Agradable: Nice, pleasant
Alguno: Some
Amable: Gentle, kind
Ancho: Wide, width
A propósito: By the way
Atención: Attention
A quién: Whom
Aún cuando: Even though
Abajo: Under
Adolescente: Adolescent
Ahora mismo: Right now
Al lado de: Next to
Ambos: Both
Antes: Before
A punto de: Ready to, almost
A través de: Through
Aquellos: Those
Aunque :Even though

Abierto: Open
A donde: Where to
A las: At (hora)
Algo : Something
Alto: Tall, high
A menos que: Unless
Apenas: Barely, merely
Apurado: In a hurry
A qué distancia: At what distance
A través de la cual: Whereby
Ayer: Yesterday
Acerca de: About
Afuera: Outside, out
Alguien: Someone, somebody
Allá: There
A menudo: Often
A pesar de: Despite
Arriba: Above, on top
A qué hora: At what time
Aún a pesar de: In spite of

Bastante:Enough, plenty
Bien: Well
Bien sea: Whether
Bueno: Good

C
Cada: Each
Cautela: Caution
Clase: Class, kind, type
Cosa: Thing
Cuando sea: Whenever
Carente: Lacking
Caliente: Hot
Ceder el paso: Yield
Cierto: Certain, true
Cómo : How
Considerando que: Whereas
Cuál: Which, What
Cuidado: Careful, mindful
Cerca: Near, fence

El método de aprendizaje South Beach para inglés conversacional

Lección No. 3 : Part E 2

Completo: Complete
Contigo: With you
Cuán lejos: How far
Culpa: Guilt
Casi: Almost, barely
Cerca de: Nearby
Con: With
Corto: Short
Cuando: When
Cualquiera: Either, anyone

D
De: By, Of
Deliberado: Willfully
Divertido: Amusing, fun
Dónde : Where
Detrás: Behind
Desviación: Deviation
De guardia: On call, on duty
De cualquier manera: Whatever
Demasiado: Enough, too much
De quién: Whose
Dividir: Divide
Donde sea: Wherever
Debajo: Underneath, under
De inmediato: Right away
Dentro: Inside
Desafortunadamente: Unfortunately
Dividir entre: Enter
Desde: Since
De buena gana: Willingly
Donde se encuentre: Whereabouts
De nuevo: Again
Desagradable: Unpleasant
Difícil: Difficult
Dividido por: Divided by
Donde quiera: Wherever
De otra manera: Somewhat
De alguna manera: Somehow

E
El: He
Ella: She
En: On, in
En caso que: In case that
En el medio: In the middle
En orden que: In order that (to)
Entonces: So
Esto: This
Específico: Specific
En algún lugar: Somewhere
En contra de: Against
En particular: In particular
Entre: Between, Enter
Esta noche: This night, tonight
Estrecho: Narrow
En buena salud: In good health
En El (la) (s): In the
En proceso: In process
En vez de: Instead of Entendido: Understood, copied
Extraño: Odd, Strange

El método de aprendizaje South Beach para inglés conversacional

LeCCIÓn No. 3 : Part E 2

En este momento: In (at) this moment
En caso de: In case of
En el hábito: In the habit
Enfrente de: In front of
En progreso: In progress
Eso: That
Esto: This

F
Fácilmente: Easily
Fiesta: Party
Factible: Feasible
Fiebre: Fever
Falla: Fault
Fin: End
Feria: Fair
Fuerte: Strong

G
Generalmente: Generally
Gracioso: Funny

Generoso: Generous Grande: Big
Gracias: Thanks

H
Habrá: There will be
Han tenido: They have had
Habría estado: There would have been
Hace: Since
Han sido: There have been
Hecho: Made in
Hasta: Until
Halar: Pull
Hasta la vista: See you later
Hay: There is
Hombre: Man
Habría sido: There would have been
Han estado: There have been
Hasta luego: See you later
Hubo: There was (were)
Habría tenido: There would have

I
Inmediatamente: Immediately

Incluído: Included
Importante: Important
Inspeccionar: Inspect
Imposible: Impossible
Interesante: Interesting
Improbable: Improbable
Izquierda: Left

J
Junio: June
Juntos: Together
Justo: Just

K
Kilo: Kilogram

L
Largo: Long
Lo último: Latest
Lo que queda: Left over
Lista: List
Luce como: Looks like
Listo: Ready, already
Luego: Afterwards, later

El método de aprendizaje South Beach para inglés conversacional

Lección No. 3 : Part E 2

M
Mañana: Morning, tomorrow
Más allá: Farther
Mientras: While
Muchacho: Boy
Muy: Very
Mantener: Maintain
Más tarde: Later
Mientras que: As long as
Mucho: A lot, too much
Más..que: More ...than
Más: More
Medio: Middle
Mitad: Half, middle
Muchos: Many
Menos... que: Less... than
Más aún: Further
Menos: Least, less
Muchacha: Young woman
Mujer: Woman
Muéstrame: Show me

N
Necesariamente: Necessary
Ninguno: Neither
Necesario: Needed
Niño: Boy
Never: Nunca
No: No, not
Niña: Girl
Noche: Night

O
O: Or
Obvio: Obvious
Otro: Other, another

P
Para: For
Perfectamente: Perfectly
Pintura: Paint
Por qué: Why
Problema: Problem
Para (Por) siempre: Forever
Pero: But

Por favor: Please
Posible: Possible
Programa: Program
Por esa razón: Wherefore, for that reason
Parece como: Looks like
Pesado; Heavy
Por: For, per
Por la razón : For the reason
Probable: Probable, possible
Próximo: Next
Partida: Departure
Pequeño: Small
Por ciento: Per cent
Por supuesto: Of course
Probablemente: Probably
Punto: Point

Q
Querido: Dear
Qué hay acerca de: What about
Quizás: Maybe, perhaps

El método de aprendizaje South Beach para inglés conversacional

LeCCIÓn No. 3 : Part E 2

R
Razonable: Reasonably
Responsable: Responsable
Relativo: Relative
Ridículo: Ridicule
Respeto: Respect
Risa: Laughter
Repita: Repeat
Responsablemente: Responsably

S
Salida: request,
departure Señora:
Mrs.
Sobrante (s): Left over (s)
Sujeto: Subject, theme
Seguro: Insurance, safe
Señorita: Ms.
Sí: Yes
Sobre: Over, above
Suficiente: Enough, sufficient
Selección: Selection
Ser nombrado: To be named

Siempre: Always, ever
Solamente: Only
Superar: Overcome
Señor: Mr.
Similar: Similar
Solo una vez: Only once

T
Tal (Tan).. como: As...as
Tarea: Task
Todavía: Yet, still
Tan pronto como sea posible:
 As soon as possible
Todo: All, Everything
También: Also, too
Tema: Subject, theme
Tan: So
Tipo: Class, kind, type
Todo el día: All day
Tarde: Afternoon, late
Tirar: Pull

U
Última (o): Last
Únicamente: Only
Un (a) (o) (s) : A
Un poco de: A bit of
Una vez: Once

V
Varios: Various
Verdad: Truth

Y
Ya: Already
Y ahora qué: And now what

El método de aprendizaje South Beach para inglés conversacional

5to. Paso de Aprendizaje

Los Posesivos y los Reflexivos

son esenciales para completar una frase

¡Practíquelos!, especialmente la pronunciación.

LeCCIÓn No. 3 : Part E 3

Reflexive / Reflexivo

Pronunciacion Espanol/Ingles   Ejemplos

			Ejemplos	
Me	Me	(Mi)	Call me	Llámame
Le	You	(Yu)	Bring you	Traerle
Le	Him	(Jim)	Take him	Llevarle
La	Her	(Jer)	Invite her	Invítarla
Nos	Us	(Os)	Get us	Búscanos
Les	You	(Yu)	Buy for you	Cómprales
Les	Them	(Dem)	Write them	Escríbeles
Lo	It	(It)	Sell it	Véndelos

Possessive / Posesivo

Ejemplos   Pronunciacion Espanol/Ingles

My home	Mi casa	Mi	My	(May)
Your car	Su coche	Su	Your	(Yur)
His son	Su hijo	Su	His	(Jis)
Her pet	Su mascota	Su	Her	(Jer)
Our boat	Nuestro barco	Nuestro	Our	(Auar)
Your dad	Vuestro padre	Vuestro	Your	(Yur)
Their idea	La idea de ellos	De ellos	Their	(Der)
Its tail	Su cola	Su	Its	(Its)

You	have	to go	to take him	home
Usted	tiene que	ir	a llevarle	a casa
Usted	le tiene	que ir	a llevar	a casa
He	can	come	to see me	later
El	puede	venir	a verme	luego
El	me puede	venir	a ver	luego
They	want	to bring	her to see	you
Ellos	la quieren	traer	a ver	le
They	are	trying	to call	today
Ellos	le están	tratando	de llamar	hoy

You	are	welcome to	our	house
Usted	es	bienvenido a	nuestra	casa
She	is	driving	my	car
Ella	está	manejando	mi	coche
He	has	to bring	my	son
El	tiene que	traer	a mi	hijo
They	want	to take	my	wife
Ellos	quieren	llevar	a mi	esposa
Today	I want	to go	to my	studio
Hoy	yo quiero	ir	a mi	estudio

El método de aprendizaje South Beach para inglés conversacional

6to. Paso de Aprendizaje

Los Verbos Infinitivos

son la base de este curso, los mismos son usados de manera casi idéntica tanto en inglés como español

¡Practíquelos!, especialmente las conjugaciones y la pronunciación

LeCCIÓn No. 4 : Part E 1

¿Qué es un Verbo Infinitivo?

1) Son aquellos que empiezan con "To" en inglés y terminan con una "R"

en español. Ejemplo:

to call	to come	to go	to eat
llamar	venir	ir	comer

2) Nunca es el 1er. verbo (no se puede conjugar)

No se puede decir en inglés	I to call	I to come	I to go	I to eat
Ni se puede decir en español.	Yo llamar	Yo venir	Yo ir	Yo comer

3) Sin embargo son siempre usados después del 1er. o 2do. Verbo.

Ejemplo:

I want	to go	to eat
Yo quiero	ir	a comer
She wants	to come	to visit
Ella quiere	venir	a visitar

El método de aprendizaje South Beach para inglés conversacional

LeCCIÓn No. 4 : Part E 2

Este curso está basado en los Verbos Infinitivos
En inglés se usan los Verbos Infinitivos todo el tiempo

I	want	to go	to eat	now
He	wants	to come	to visit	you

Los Hispanos también usamos los Verbos Infinitivos
Todo el tiempo y ¡de la misma manera que ellos!

I	want	to go	to eat	now
Yo	quiero	ir	a comer	ahora
He	wants	to come	to visit	you
El	quiere	venir	a visitar	le

SONRÍA ☺ Ambas frases parecen un espejo, la una de la otra, con la excepción de la vocal "a" que nosotros utilizamos antes del segundo verbo infinitivo.

El método de aprendizaje South Beach para inglés conversacional

LeCCIÓn No. 4 : Part E 3

Este curso está basado en los **Verbos Infinitivos**
¡Aquí tiene más ejemplos!

I	**have**	**to take**	**you**	**She**	**wants**	**to watch TV**	**'til midnight**
Yo	tengo que	llevar	le	Ella	quiere	mirar TV	hasta la medianoche
You	**have**	**to bring**	**him**	**We**	**want**	**to go to shop**	**at noon**
Usted	tiene que	traer	le	Nosotros	queremos	ir a comprar	al mediodía
He	**has**	**to go to see**	**you**	**They**	**want**	**to give you**	**a surprise**
El	tiene que	ir a ver	le	Ellos	quieren	dar le	una sorpresa
We	**have**	**to try to get**	**there**	**You**	**want**	**to do him**	**a lot of good**
Nosotros	tenemos que	tratar de llegar	allá	Usted	quiere	hacer le	mucho bien

Las ocho frases son un espejo la una de la otra, palabra por palabra, con la excepción de la palabra "que", la cual se utiliza en español cuando el verbo tener se usa para expresar deber o responsabilidad, (ejemplo: Yo me tengo "que" ir), al contrario de cuando se utiliza para describir posesión o propiedad (ejemplo: Yo tengo una familia) y la letra "a" que se utiliza en español después del primer verbo, (ejemplo: Yo me tengo que ir "a" dormir).

Los dos idiomas cuando se hablan correctamente, ¡se hablan de la misma y exacta manera!

El método de aprendizaje South Beach para inglés conversacional

LeCCIÓn No. 4 : Part E 3

**Lo único que usted necesita para poder conversar en inglés son
los Verbos Infinitivos los cuales son la base de este método de aprendizaje.**

- Los verbos infinitivos se usan de la misma manera y casi siempre en el mismo lugar en una oración, tanto en inglés como español.

- Los verbos infinitivos nunca son el primer verbo en una oración: I   want   to have
                                                                                                                                          Yo quiero   tener

- Los verbos infinitivos empiezan con To en inglés: To have
      Y terminan en R en español: Tener

- Los verbos infinitivos no pueden ser conjugados: To have
                                                                                                     Yo tener

- Los verbos infinitivos continúan siendo usados de manera   I   want   to go   to eat
  Infinita en las oraciones. Ahí los dos idiomas son idénticos o   Yo quiero   ir   a comer
                                                                                                                                 I   want   to go   to sleep
- El segundo verbo infinitivo en una frase en español es   Yo quiero   ir   a dormir
  siempre precedido por la letra "a"

- Los verbos infinitivos nos permiten conversar en inglés a través de cuatro formatos en fórmula: (1) Gerundio-acción, (2) Pasado participio, (3) Futuro y (4) Condicional.

El método de aprendizaje South Beach para inglés conversacional

LeCCIÓn No. 4 : Part E 4

En la próxima página
usted encontrará una
lista de:

Verbos Infinitivos
Infinitive Verbs

Estúdielos, léalos, pronúncielos varias veces
hasta que los memorice,
y se dará cuenta que todos ellos (bueno, casi todos)

Terminan en_____R en español
Empiezan en To_____en inglés

El método de aprendizaje South Beach para inglés conversacional

LeCCIÓn No. 4 : Part E 4

A
Abrir: To open
Abrazar: To hug
Aceptar: To accept
Acertar: To be right
Adquirir: To acquire
Agradecer: To thank
Amar: To love
Anunciar: To announce
Aprender: To learn
Aprobar: To approve
Arreglar: To arrange
Asistir: To assist
Aumentar: To increase
Averiguar: To find out
Ayudar: To help

B
Bailar: To dance
Beber: To drink
Borrar: To erase
Bostezar: To yawn
Buscar: To seek, to search

C
Caber: To fit
Caer: To fall
Calentar: To heat
Caminar: To walk
Cancelar: To nix
Causar: To cause
Cobrar: To collect
Cocinar: To cook
Conducir: To drive
Conseguir: To get
Construir: To build
Convertir: To become
Cerrar: To close, to zip
Completar: To complete
Comprar: To buy, to purchase
Comer: To eat
Copiar: To copy
Corregir: To correct
Correr: To run
Creer: To believe
Crecer: To grow
Cumplir: To keep

D
Dar: To give
Darse cuenta: To realize
Deber: Must, to owe (deuda)
Debería: Should
Decir: To say, to tell
Dejar: To let, to leave, to abandon
Descansar: To rest
Desear: To wish
Discutir: To argue, To discuss
Dormir: To sleep
Dudar: To doubt
Devengar: To earn

E
Empezar: To start, To begin
Empujar: To push
Encontrar: To find
Enseñar: To teach
Enviar: To send
Entender: To understand
Entrar: To enter
Escoger (Elegir): To pick
Escribir: To write
Esperar: To wait
Estar: To be
Estar agradecido: To be thankful
Estar molesto: To be angry
Estar equivocado: To be wrong
Estudiar: To study

G
Ganar: To earn
Ganar: To win
Golpear: To hit

Gustar: To like

H
Haber: To have
Hablar: To talk
Hablar: To speak
Hacer: To do
Hacer: to make
Halar: To pull

I
Incluir: To include
Informar: To inform
Insistir: To insist
Invitar: To invite
Ir: To go
Ir de compras: To shop

J
Jugar: To play (a game, gamble)

L
Lavar: To wash
Leer: To read
Limpiar: To clean

El método de aprendizaje South Beach para inglés conversacional

LeCCIÓn No. 4 : Part E 4

Llamar: To call
Llegar: To arrive
Llevar: To take
Llorar: To cry
Lograr: To get

M
Manejar: To drive Mover:
To move Mejorar: To
improve Mantener: To keep
up Mostrar: To show Mirar:
To watch, to look

N
Nombrar: To name
Necesitar: To need

O
Obedecer: To obey
Observar: To observe
Obtener: To get Ofrecer:
To offer Olvidar: To forget
Ordenar: To order

P
Pagar: To pay
Parecer: To look
Partir: To leave, to depart
Pasar: To happen
Pedir: To ask
Pedir prestado: To borrow
Pensar: To think
Perder: To lose
Perdonar: To forgive
Perdonar: To pardon
Permitir: To allow
Poder: Can, may
Podría: Could, may
Preguntar: To ask
Presentar: To present
Prestar: To lend Poner:
To put Poseer: To own

Q
Querer: To want

R
Rechazar: To reject
Recibir: To get
Recibir: To greet

Recordar: To remember
Recoger: To return
Reir: To laugh
Repetir: To repeat
Respetar: to respect
Responder: To answer
Responder: To reply
Reusar: To refuse

S
Saber: To know
Salir: To exit
Salvar: To save
Saltar: To jump
Satisfacer: To satisfy
Seguir: To follow
Sentar: To sit
Sentir: To feel
Ser: To be
Solicitar: To request
Solucionar: To solve
Sonreir: To smile

T
Temer: To fear
Tener: To have
Tener que: To have to

Terminar: To finish
Trabajar: To work
Traer: To bring
Tomar: To take
Tratar: To try
Trotar: To trot
Tocar: To touch
Tocar: To play (instrument)

U
Unir: To join
Usar: To use, to wear
Utilizar: To utilize

V
Valorar: To value
Vender: To sell
Venir: To come
Ver: To see
Vestir: To dress
Viajar: To travel
Visitar: To visit
Vivir: To live

W

El método de aprendizaje South Beach para inglés conversacional

7mo. Paso de Aprendizaje

Los 4 Verbos "Gatillo"

le permiten iniciar cualquier conversación básica

Practíquelos, especialmente las conjugaciones Y la pronunciación

LeCCIÓn 5, 6, 7, 8

Los siguientes 4 verbos gatillo le permiten iniciar
la mayor parte de las conversaciones

Lección No. 5	Lección No. 6
To be (Tu bi) Ser/Estar	To have (To jav) Tener/ Haber
Lección No. 7	Lección No.8
To want (Tu guant) Querer	Can (kan) Poder

El método de aprendizaje South Beach para inglés conversacional

Lección No. 5 : Part E 1

El 1er. Verbo Gatillo es "To Be" (Tu Bi)

En español significa "Ser o Estar", es decir que tiene dos significados

Primero estudiaremos el verbo "Ser"

El verbo "Ser" en español describe una situación casi-permanente

Ejemplos usando el verbo "Ser"

To be (tu bi)				I am tall			He is a policeman		
I	(ai)	**am**	(am)	Yo	soy	alto	El	es	un policía
You	(yu)	**are**	(ar)	**She**	**is**	**smart**	**You**	**are**	**single**
He	(hi)	**is**	(is)	Ella	es	lista	Usted	es	soltero
She	(she)	**is**	(is)	**They**	**are**	**fanatics**	**He**	**is**	**late**
We	(gui)	**are**	(ar)	Ellos	son	fanáticos	El	está	tarde
They	(dei)	**are**	(ar)	**It**	**is**	**late**	**She**	**is**	**beautiful**
it	(it)	**is**	(is)	Es		tarde	Ella	es	bella

LeCCIÓn No. 5 : Part E 2

El 1er. Verbo Gatillo es "To Be" (Tu Bi)
En español significa "Ser o Estar", es decir que tiene dos significados Ahora estudiaremos el verbo "Estar": El verbo "Estar" en español describe una situación que no es permanente sino más bien transitoria, pero lo más importante que debemos notar es que en inglés ¡Estar y Ser se dicen IGUAL!

Ejemplos usando el verbo "Ser"								
To be (tu bi)			**I**	**am**	**angry**	**They**	**are**	**ready**
I	(ai)	**am** (am)	Yo	estoy	molesto	Ellos	están	listos
You	(yu)	**are** (ar)	**You**	**are**	**late**	**She**	**is**	**sick**
He	(hi)	**is** (is)	Usted	está	tarde	Ella	está	enferma
She	(she)	**is** (is)	**He**	**is**	**tired**	**You**	**are**	**out**
We	(gui)	**are** (ar)	El	está	cansado	Usted	está	afuera
They	(dei)	**are** (ar)	**She**	**is**	**wrong**	**It**	**is**	**right**
it	(it)	**is** (is)	Ella	esta	equivocada	Es	lo	correcto

El método de aprendizaje South Beach para inglés conversacional

Lección No. 5 : Part E 3

Los Verbos "Gatillo" To be (tu bi)

Situación casi permanente	Situación temporal
I am a good player Yo soy un buen jugador	**I am eating early each day** Yo estoy comiendo temprano cada día
I am a great person Yo soy una gran persona	**I am waiting for you now** Yo estoy esperando por usted ahora
You are a good man Usted es un buen hombre	**You are tired every day** Usted está cansado todos los días
You are a disgusting person Usted es una persona desagradable	**You are upset about the game** Usted está molesto acerca del juego
He is an excellent student El es un estudiante excelente	**He is taking them to the airport** El los está llevando al aeropuerto
He is a fantastic cook El es un cocinero fantástico	**He is going to visit you this weekend** El está yendo a visitarle este fin de semana
We are always here for you Nosotros estamos siempre aquí para usted	**She is coming home for Thanksgiving** Ella está viniendo a casa en Acción de Gracias
We are the same people Nosotros somos la misma gente	**We are thinking about you** Nosotros estamos pensando acerca de usted
You are a winning team Ustedes son un equipo ganador	**You are frustrated by the whole situation** Usted está frustrado por toda la situación
You are never on time Ustedes nunca están a tiempo	**They are very tired after the trip** Ellos están muy cansados después del viaje
They are the best in town Ellos son los mejores en la ciudad	**It is getting late** Se está haciendo tarde
They are the worst there is Ellos son lo peor que hay	**We are doing our homework** Nosotros estamos haciendo nuestra tarea
It is better if you don't come Es mejor si usted no viene	**She is trying to finish her task today** Ella está tratando de finalizar su tarea hoy

El método de aprendizaje South Beach para inglés conversacional

LeCCIÓn No. 6 : Part E 1

El 2do. Verbo Gatillo es "To Have" (Tu jav)
En español significa "Tener o Haber", es decir que tiene dos significados

Existen dos verbos "Tener" en español

1) Tener, cuando describe propiedad o posesión

2) Tener que, cuando describe deber o responsabilidad Es

importante hacer notar que en inglés ¡Ambos se dicen igual!

Ejemplos usando el verbo "To have"		
To have (tu jav)	**Describiendo propiedad**	**Describiendo responsabilidad**
I (ai) **have** (jav)	**I have an automobile** Yo tengo un coche	**I have to go to eat** Yo tengo "que" ir a comer
You (yu) **have** (jav)	**He has an extended family** El tiene una familia numerosa	**I have to talk with him** Yo tengo "que" hablar con él
He (hi) **has** (jas)		
She (she) **has** (jas)	**You have a problem** Usted tiene un problema	**He has to take you home** El tiene "que" llevarle a casa
We (gui) **have** (jav)	**She has a headache** Ella tiene un dolor de cabeza	**We have to see you** Nosotros tenemos"que" verle
They (dei) **have** (jav)		
You (yu) **have** (jav)	**You have a visitor** Usted tiene un visitante	**He has to live now** Ella se tiene"que" ir ahora
It (it) **has** (jas)		

El método de aprendizaje South Beach para inglés conversacional

Lección No. 6 : Part E 2

El 2do. Verbo Gatillo es "To Have" (Tu jav)
En español significa "Tener o Haber", es decir que tiene dos significados

Estudiemos ahora el 2do. significado del verbo To Have (To Jav)
En español el verbo "To Have" también significa Haber, y lo utilizamos para hablar en pasado participio, en español casi todos estos verbos terminan en "ido o ado"

Ejemplos usando el verbo "To have" (tu jav) como "Haber" en Pasado Participio

To have (tu jav)			
I (ai) **have** (jav)	I have gotten mail today Yo he recibido correo hoy	I have gone to eat Yo he ido a comer
You (yu) **have** (jav)	You have taken a long time Usted ha tomado mucho tiempo	You have not called me Usted no me ha llamado
He (hi) **has** (jas) **She** (she) **has** (jas)	She has slept in the morning Ella ha dormido en la mañana	He has come to see me El ha venido a verme
We (gui) **have** (jav)	They have studied all day Ellos han estudiado todo el día	She has taken me home Ella me ha llevado a casa
You (yu) **have** (jav)	They have cooked all morning Ellos han cocinado toda la mañana	I have not gone to sleep Yo no me he ido a dormir
They (dei) **have** (jav) **It** (it) **has** (jas)	He has been running all afternoon El ha estado corriendo toda la tarde	They have not watched TV Ellos no han mirado TV

El método de aprendizaje South Beach para inglés conversacional

LeCCIÓn No. 6 : Part E 3

Aquí hay múltiples ejemplos del verbo "To Have"
cuando es utilizado como "Haber" en inglés

To Have: Haber

I have done Yo he hecho	**They have studied** Ellos han estudiado	**You have understood** Usted ha entendido
I have gotten Yo he recibido	**I have run** Yo he corrido	**He has written** El ha escrito
I have taken Yo he llevado	**She has walked** Ella ha caminado	**I have healed** Yo me he curado
You have cooked Yo he cocinado	**They have called** Ellos han llamado	**You have improved** Usted ha mejorado
He has waited El ha esperado	**I have spoken** Yo he hablado	**They have thought** Ellos han pensado
She has gone Ella ha ido	**I have bought it** Yo lo he comprado	**You have brought it** Usted lo ha traído
She has seen Ella ha visto	**She has shopped** Ella ha ido de compras	**She has bathed** Ella se ha bañado

El método de aprendizaje South Beach para inglés conversacional

LeCCIÓn No. 6 : Part E 3

Tener	Tener que	Pasado Participio
I have a great family	**I have to see you tomorrow**	**I have received mail today**
Yo tengo una gran familia	Yo tengo que verle mañana	Yo he recibido correo hoy
I have a headache	**I have to come to see you**	**I have slept well yesterday night**
Yo tengo dolor de cabeza	Yo tengo que venir a verle	Yo he dormido bien anoche
You have four good kids	**You have to go to eat**	**Yo have not done your work**
Usted tiene cuatro hijos buenos	Usted tiene que ir a comer	Usted no ha hecho su trabajo
I have a good job	**I have to meet with him today**	**I have seen her early today**
Yo tengo un buen trabajo	Yo tengo que reunirme con el hoy	Yo la he visto hoy temprano
He has problems with her	**He has to bring him the food**	**He has made a big mistake**
El tiene problemas con ella	El tiene que traerle la comida	El ha cometido un gran error
They have a great life	**They have to hurry up**	**They have eaten a lot today**
Ellos tienen una gran vida	Ellos se tienen que apurar	Ellos han comido mucho hoy
You have a lot of luck	**You have to finish the project**	**We have sent her to school**
Ustedes tiene mucha suerte	Usted tiene que terminar el proyecto	Nosotros la hemos enviado a la escuela
I have a rough road ahead	**We have to start moving**	**You have been absent lately**
Yo tengo un camino difícil por delante	Nosotros tenemos que comenzar a movernos	Ustedes han estado ausentes ultimamente
You have a lot of luck	**She has to pay attention**	**She has bought new clothes**
Ustedes tiene mucha suerte	Ella tiene que poner atención	Ella ha comprado ropa nueva
She has a brand new car	**It has to be fixed**	**It has been repaired already**
Ella tiene un coche nuevo	Tiene que ser reparado	Ya ha sido reparado
It has a broken light	**I have to start all over again**	**I have been thinking about it**
Tiene una luz rota	Yo tengo que empezar de nuevo	Yo he estado pensando en ello

El método de aprendizaje South Beach para inglés conversacional

LeCCIÓn No. 7 : Part E 1

El 3er. Verbo Gatillo es "To Want" (Tu guant)
En español significa "Querer", y se usa de dos formas distintas
Al igual que en español el verbo "To Want" se utiliza en inglés para:
1) Expresar un deseo con el verbo "Querer" (To Want).
2) Expresar una orden con el verbo "Querer que" (To Want).

Ejemplos: Tal como en inglés el verbo "Querer" se usa pirncipalmente de dos maneras		
To want (tu guant) **I** (ai) **want** (guant)	**Para expresar deseo**	**Para dar órdenes o pedir**
You (yu) **want** (guant)	**I want to go to sleep** Yo me quiero ir a dormir	**I want you to go to eat** Yo quiero que usted vaya comer
He (hi) **wants** (guants) **She** (she) **wants** (guants)	**I want to learn Spanish** Yo quiero aprender español	**He wants you to write to him** El quiere que usted le escriba
We (gui) **want** (guant) **You** (yu) **want** (guant)	**She wants to cook for you** Ella quiere cocinarle a ustedes	**We want you to think about it** Queremos que lo piense
They (dei) **want** (guant) **It** (it) **wants** (guants)	**They want to take you home** Ellos quieren llevarle a casa	**I want you to bring me the check** Yo quiero que me traiga la cuenta

El método de aprendizaje South Beach para inglés conversacional

LeCCIÓn No. 7 : Part E 2

To want (tu guant)		To want (tu guant)
Desire / Wish **Desear/Querer**	Ejemplos	**Command / Order** **Comando/ Orden**
I want to take you to the movies Yo quiero llevarle al cine		**I want that you stop calling me** Yo quiero que usted pare de llamarme
I want to go shopping today after lunch Yo quiero ir de compras hoy después de comer		**I want that you think about it carefully** Yo quiero que lo piense con cuidado
You want me to bring you anything? ¿Usted quiere que le traiga alguna cosa?		**Do you want that we get him ready?** ¿Usted quiere que lo tengamos listo?
He wants to buy a brand new pair of shoes El quiere comprar un par de zapatos nuevos		**He wants that you call him today at 2 p.m.** El quiere que usted lo llame hoy a las 2 p.m.
She wants to try to find a new job Ella quiere tratar de conseguir un trabajo nuevo		**She wants me not to bother her anymore** Ella quiere que yo no la moleste más

El método de aprendizaje South Beach para inglés conversacional

LeCCIÓn No. 8 : Part E 1

El 4to. Verbo Gatillo es "Can" (kan)

En español significa "Poder"

To can (tu can)		
I (ai) **can** (kan) **You** (yu) **can** (kan)	**I can see you late**r Yo puedo verle luego	**He can come at noon** El puede venir al mediodía
He (hi) **can** (kan) **She** (she) **can** (kan)	**She can go to see him** Ella puede ir a verle	**You can do it** Usted puede hacerlo
We (gui) **can** (kan) **You** (yu) **can** (kan)	**They can take you home** Ellos pueden llevarle a casa	**You can come in** Usted puede entrar
They (dei) **can** (kan) **It** (it) **can** (kan)	**He can come tomorrow** El puede venir mañana	**I can call you later** Yo puedo llamarle luego

El método de aprendizaje South Beach para inglés conversacional

LeCCIÓn No. 8 : Part E 2

Ejemplos: Can

I can come to see you this weekend
Yo puedo venir a verle éste fin de semana

I can call you every night at 8 p.m.
Yo puedo llamarle todas las noches a las 8 p.m.

He can take them to the park tomorrow at 4
El puede llevarles al parque mañana a las 4

She can not eat chicken
Ella no puede comer pollo

We can work together to solve the problem
Nosotros podemos trabajar juntos para resolver el problema

He can prepare for the test this week
El puede prepararse para el examen esta semana

You can bring them over to spend the day here
Usted puede traerlos a pasar el día aquí

You can go to the movies with them
Usted puede ir al cine con ellos

You can call me after lunch
Usted puede llamarme después del almuerzo

They can complain all they want, it won't make a difference
Ellos pueden protestar todo lo que quieran pero no hará diferencia

El método de aprendizaje South Beach para inglés conversacional

LeCCIÓn No. 9 : Part E 1

Ok. Usemos ahora los Pronombres, los cuatro Verbos Gatillo, las Palabras Mágicas
y los Verbos Infinitivos adicionales para construir más Oraciones y Frases

Pronombres

Yo	I	(ai)
Usted	You	(yu)
El	He	(ji)
Ella	She	(shi)
Nosotros	We	(gui)
Ustedes	You	(yu)
Ellos	They	(dei)
Eso/esto	It	(it)

Los 4 Verbos Gatillo

To Be	(tu bi)	Ser
To Be	(tu bi)	Estar
To Have	(tu jav)	Tener
To Have	(tu jav)	Haber
To Want	(tu guant)	Querer
Can	(kan)	Poder

Ejemplos

I have to go to call her
Yo tengo que ir a llamarla

I want to take you to dinner
Yo quiero llevarle a cenar

He can wait for you at noon
El puede esperar por usted al mediodía

I have to go to take notes
Yo tengo que ir a tomar notas

I can go to see you tomorrow
Yo puedo ir a verle mañana

We can cook rather quickly
Nosotros podemos cocinar muy rápido

We have to wait for her
Nosotros tenemos que esperar por ella

I want to come to see you
Yo quiero venir a verle

You can go to sleep
Usted puede irse a dormir

She wants to cook for you
Ella quiere cocinarle

I have to run to go to see him
Yo tengo que correr para ir a verle

They can come to run tonight
Ellos pueden venir a correr esta noche

He has to call her soon
El tiene que llamarla pronto

El método de aprendizaje South Beach para inglés conversacional

Lección No. 9 : Part E 2

Verbos Gatillo Adicionales: **Ejemplos**

To Go	**ir** (ihr)	
To Come	**Venir** (vehneer)	
To Take	**Tomar** (tohmar)	
To Buy	**Comprar** (comprar)	
To Cook	**Cocinar** (cocinar)	
To Wait	**Esperar** (esperar)	
To Run	**Correr** (correr)	
To Watch	**Mirar** (mirahr)	
To See	**Ver** (Vehr)	
To Give	**Dar** (Dahr)	
To Get	**Recibir** (Receebir)	
To Get	**Obtener** (Obtener)	
To Walk	**Caminar** (Caminar)	
To Write	**Escribir** (Escribir)	
To Read	**Leer** (Lehehr)	

You have to come to see her
Usted tiene que venir a verla
You can come to watch TV later
Usted puede venir a ver TV luego
She wants you to call soon
Ella quiere que la llame pronto
He can read pretty well
El puede leer muy bien
They have to run today
Ellos tienen que correr hoy
She wants to run every morning
Ella quiere correr todas las mañanas
They can take you to the airport now
Ellos pueden llevarle al aeropuerto ahora
You can go to buy groceries at three
Nosotros podemos comprar comida a las tres

He has to get mail this week
El tiene que recibir correo esta semana
He has to go to get his ID
El tiene que ir a obtener su ID
He has to learn to write often
El tiene que aprender a escribir a menudo

El método de aprendizaje South Beach para inglés conversacional

LeCCIÓn No. 9 : Part E 3

Ahora construyamos frases con lo que hemos aprendido

I have to be a good father
Yo tengo que ser un buen padre

I want to be fair
Yo quiero ser justo

I can be often late
Yo puedo estar tarde a menudo

You have to be persistent
Usted tiene que ser persistente

You want to be the best
Usted quiere ser el major

You can be the last to come in
Usted puede ser el último en venir

We have to be polite
Nosotros tenemos que ser educados

We want to be the best
Nosotros queremos ser los mejores

We can be of great help to you
Nosotros le podemos ser de gran ayuda

I have to be there on time
Yo tengo que estar allí a tiempo

I want to be present
Yo quiero estar presente

I can be there at two
Yo puedo estar allá a las dos

You have to be alert all the time
Usted tiene que estar alerta todo el tiempo

You want to be ahead of the curve
Usted quiere estar adelante de la curva

You can have a lot of trouble soon
Ustedes pueden tener muchos problemas pronto

We have to be waiting for him at the gate
Nosotros tenemos que estar esperándole en la Puerta

He can be available later
El puede estar disponible luego

He has to be patient
El tiene que ser paciente

He wants to be like his father
El quiere ser como su padre

He can be a very good team mate
El puede ser un gran miembro del equipo

We want to be ready for him
Nosotros queremos estar listos para él

We can be in the losing end
Nosotros podemos estar en el lado perdedor

He has to be devastated
El tiene que estar devastado

He wants to be permanently on vacations
El quiere estar de vacaciones permanentemente

El método de aprendizaje South Beach para inglés conversacional

LeCCIÓn No. 9 : Part E 4

Los Verbos Infinitivos/Los Cuatro Verbos Gatillo						
Verbos infinitivos		**To Be**	**To Want**	**To Have**	**Can**	**Will**
Pronombre		Ser/Estar	Querer	Tener/ Haber	Poder	Ir a
Yo	I (ai)	am (am)	want (guant)	have (jav)	can (kan)	will (guil)
Usted	You (yu)	are (ar)	want (guant)	have (jav)	can (kan)	will (guil)
El	He (ji)	is (is)	wants (guants)	has (jas)	can (kan)	will (guil)
Ella	She (shi)	is (is)	wants (guants)	has (jas)	can (kan)	will (guil)
Nosotros (nohsohtrohs)	We (gui)	are (ar)	want (guant)	have (jav)	can (kan)	will (guil)
Ustedes (uhstehdehs)	You (yu)	are (ar)	want (guant)	have (jav)	can (kan)	will (guil)
Ellos (ehyohs)	They (dei)	are (ar)	want (guant)	have (jav)	can (kan)	will (guil)
Eso/Esto (ehsoh/ ehstoh)	It (it)	is (is)	wants (guants)	has (jas)	can (kan)	will (guil)

El método de aprendizaje South Beach para inglés conversacional

8avo. Paso de Aprendizaje

Los 4 formatos en fórmula

(Plantillas)
Le permiten conversar en Gerundio (acción) Participio Pasado, Futuro Condicional usando únicamente "Verbos Infinitivos"

Practíquelos, especialmente las conjugaciones y (la pronunciación)

1. Gerundio/ Gerund (Acción):

Gerundio/ Gerund (Acción)
INGLÉS: To be + Verbo termina "ing"
ESPAÑOL: Estar + Verbo termina en "iendo" o "ando".
Cómo convertir un:
Verbo Infinitivo" en inglés a gerundio
To Walk :Elimine "To" y añada "ing" Walking
Verbo Infinitivo" en español a gerundio
Caminar: Elimine la "r" y añada "ando"Caminando
Ejemplo: To Walk = Caminar (Verbo Infinitivo)
I am walking to eat
Yo estoy caminando a comer

Lección No. 10 : Part E 1

English To Be + El verbo termina en **"ing"**
Spanish Estar + El verbo termina <u>**iendo**</u> o <u>**ando**</u>

- En inglés cuando se habla en Gerundio refiere a "acción".
- Y cuando se usa de esta manera el verbo "To Be" es seguido siempre por un verbo terminado en "ing".
- En español es exactamente lo mismo, los hispanos usan el verbo "Estar" (To Be) seguido siempre de un verbo terminado en iendo o ando.

Ejemplo:
<u>**To call :   I   am   calling   you   tonight**</u>
<u>Llamar :   Yo estoy llamándole esta noche</u>

En fin de cuentas ing. En inglés es endo/ando en español

Para convertir un verbo infinitivo en Gerundio:
<u>En inglés hacemos lo siguiente: To call------calling (eliminar el "To" añadir "ing").</u>
<u>En español hacemos lo siguiente: Llamar------llamando (eliminar la "r" añadir "iendo" o "ando").</u>

Nota: <u>"To be" en español es o "Ser" o "Estar".</u> Cuando se habla en Gerundio en español solo se puede hacer usando el verbo "Estar". Ejemplo: <u>Yo estoy</u> comiendo.

LeCCIÓn No. 10 : Part E 2

Ejemplos:

Gerundio

I am calling you now
Yo estoy llamándole ahora
noche

I am studying all morning
Yo estoy estudiando toda la mañana

I am waiting at the house
Yo estoy esperando en la casa

I am writing to you every week
Yo estoy escribiéndole cada semana
I am trying to visit you
Yo estoy tratando de visitarle
I am learning to speak Spanish
Yo estoy aprendiendo a hablar
español

I am watching hispanic TV
Yo estoy viendo la TV en español

They are calling him today
Ellos están llamándole hoy

They are studying today
Ellos están estudiando hoy

We are waiting for you
Ellos están esperando por usted

They are writing every other week
Ellos están escribiendo cada dos
semanas
She is trying to visit us
Ella está tratando de visitarnos
She is learning about the country
Ella está aprendiendo acerca
del país

You are watching her grow
Usted está mirándola crecer

They are calling tonight
Ellos están llamándole esta

She is studying now
Ella está estudiando ahora

You are waiting in vain
Usted está esperando en vano

He is writing often
El está escribiendo a menudo

They are trying to call
Ellos están tratando de llamar

He is learning the basic
El está aprendiendo lo básico

He is watching the game
El está mirando el juego

Verbos Infinitvos:

To Call : Llamar   To Study :Estudiar   To Wait :Esperar   To Write: Escribir   To Try: Tratar
To Learn: Aprender   To Watch: Mirar

El método de aprendizaje South Beach para inglés conversacional

2. Participio/Participle (Pasado Participio)

	Participio/Participle (Pasado Participio) INGLÉS: To have + verbo en Participio ESPAÑOL: **Cómo convertir un:** Yo he **Verbo Infinitivo a Participio,** Usted ha elimine la "r" y añada "ido" El ha o "ado Ella ha Nosotros hemos **Ejemplo:** Ustedes han To Wait = Esperar (Verbo Infinitivo) Ellos han **I have been waiting for you** Eso/Esto ha Yo he estado esperando por usted

El método de aprendizaje South Beach para inglés conversacional

LeCCIÓn No. 11 : Part E 1

Inglés: To have --- Español: Haber		Ejemplos en Pasado participio
I have (jav) You have (jav) He has (jas) She has (jas) We have (jav) You have (jav) They have(jav) It has (jas)	**To take: I have taken her home** Llevar : Yo la he llevado a casa	**To wait: They have been waiting for you** Esperar: Ellos han estado esperando por usted
	To eat: He has eaten at 12 Comer: El ha comido a las 12	**To wash: She has been washing all morning** Lavar: Ella ha estado lavando toda la mañana
	To learn: They have learned to read Aprender: Ellos han aprendido a leer	**To ask: He has been asking for you** Preguntar: El ha estado preguntando por usted
	To talk: She has talked to him Hablar: Ella ha hablado con él	**To cook: They have been cooking today** Cocinar: Ellos han estado cocinando hoy
	To study: We have studied Estudiar: Nosotros hemos estudiado	**To walk: We have walked** Caminar: Nosotros hemos caminado
	To get: They have gotten no mail Recibir: Ellos no han recibido correo	**To think: You have thought about it** Pensar : Usted ha pensado acerca de eso
	To go: I have gone to see her Ir : Yo he ido a verla	**To come: You have been coming every year** Venir: Usted ha estado viniendo cada año
	To bring: He has brought a friend Traer: El ha traído una amiga	**To win: We have been winning more** Ganar: Nosotros hemos estado ganando más
	To listen: She has listened to him Escuchar: Ella le ha escuchado	**To buy: I have been buying lots of vitamins** Comprar: Yo he estado comprando muchas vitaminas
Verbos en Pasado Participio vea lista adjunta		

El método de aprendizaje South Beach para inglés conversacional

Lección No. 11 : Part E 2

Past Participle (Verbs)/(Verbos) Pasado Participle

Been *Sido*	**Been** *Estado*	**Arrived** *Llegado*	**Washed** *Lavado*	**Cooled** *Enfriado*	**Packed** *Empacado*	**Written** *Escrito*	**Fought** *Peleado*
Come *Venido*	**Talked** *Hablado*	**Calculated** *Calculado*	**Explained** *Explicado*	**Looked** *Mirado*	**Brought** *Traído*	**Replied** *Respondido*	**Thought** *Pensado*
Gotten *Recibido*	**Taken** *Lleva do/ Tomado*	**Seen** *Visto*	**Repeated** *Repetido*	**Appealed** *Apelado*	**Needed** *Necesitado*	**Heated** *Calentado*	**Watched** *Mirado*
Ran *Corrido*	**Cleaned** *Limpiado*	**Called** *Llamado*	**Had** *Tenido*	**Finished** *Finalizado*	**Disputed** *Disputado*	**Cooked** *Cocinado*	**Replied** *Respondido*
Done *Hecho*	**Failed** *Fallado*	**Given** *Dado*	**Listened** *Escuchado*	**Accepted** *Aceptado*	**Built** *Construído*	**Traveled** *Viajado*	**Grabbed** *Agarrado*
Wished *Deseado*	**Made** *Hecho*	**Walked** *Caminado*	**Bought** *Comprado*	**Asked** *Preguntado*	**Wanted** *Querido*	**Realized** *Dado cuenta*	**Started** *Empezado*
Remembered *Recordado*	**Baked** *Horneado*	**Put** *Puesto*	**Sat** *Sentado*	**Read** *Leído*	**Eaten** *Comido*	**Gone** *Ido*	**Enjoyed** *Disfrutado*
Fried *Frito*	**Heard** *Escuchado*	**Lost** *Perdido*	**Liked** *Gustado*	**Stood** *Parado*	**Bathed** *Bañado*	**Said** *Dicho*	**Searched** *Buscado*
Slept *Dormido*	**Agreed** *Acordado*	**Exited** *Salido*	**Left** *Dejado*	**Loved** *Amado*	**Woken** *Despertado*	**Layed** *Dejado*	**Saddened** *Entristecido*
Questioned *Preguntado*	**Entered** *Introducido*	**Hurt** *Herido*	**Found** *Encontrado*	**Flown** *Volado*	**Won** *Ganado*	**Cried** *Llorado*	**Shipped** *Enviado*
Ordered *Ordenado*	**Boiled** *Hervido*	**Dreamed** *Soñado*	**Drank** *Bebido*	**Paid** *Pagado*	**Swam** *Nadado*	**Waited** *Esperado*	**Started** *Empezado*
Answered *Respondido*	**Understood** *Entendido*	**Argued** *Discutido*	**Jumped** *Saltado*	**Forgotten** *Olvidado*	**Arrived** *Llegado*	**Dried** *Secado*	**Shown** *Mostrado*

El método de aprendizaje South Beach para inglés conversacional

3. Future/ Futuro

Future/ Futuro

INGLÉS: Will + Verbo infinitivo.
ESPAÑOL: Yo voy a + Verbo Infinitivo.

Yo voy a	I will
Usted va a	You will
El va a	He will
Ella va a	She will
Nosotros vamos a	We will
Ustedes van a	You will
Ellos van a	They will
Eso/esto va a	It will

Ejemplo: To go = Ir To eat = Comer (Verbos infinitivos)

I will go to eat later
Yo voy a ir a comer después

Lección No. 12 : Part E 1

	Ejemplo	
Inglés: Pronombre + verbo infinitivo Español:	I will go to run later Yo voy a ir a correr después	They will go to visit you soon Ellos van a venir a visitarle pronto
I will (guil)	**You will not finish** Usted no va a terminar	**I will study all day** Yo voy a estudiar todo el día
You will		
He will	**She will call you later** Ella va a llamarle luego	**They will get your food** Ellos van a traerle la comida
She will		
We will +verbo infinitivo	**You will take me home** Usted va a llevarme a casa	**He will cook for you today** El va a cocinarle hoy
You will		
They will	**He will wait for you at 12** El le va a esperar a las doce	**He will fly out at 3** El va a volar a las 3
	He will bring you lunch at 1 El le va a traer el almuerzo a la 1	**You will not be on time** Usted no va a estar a tiempo

El método de aprendizaje South Beach para inglés conversacional

4. Conditional/ Condicional

Conditional/ Condicional

INGLÉS: Could + Verbo infinitivo

   Should

    Would

ESPAÑOL: Verbo infinitivo + "ia" o "iera"

Ejemplo: To go = Ir

   To run = Correr (Verbos in initivos)

I would go to run if you would come with me

Yo iría a correr si usted viniera conmigo

Lección No. 13 : Part E 1

	Inglés Condic.	Español Condicional
¿Qué es un verbo condicional? Aquél que refleje una condición: en inglés cualquier verbo que termine en "ould", en español cualquier verbo que termine en "ia" o "iera" ¿Cómo convertir un verbo en inglés al condicional? Simplemente añada "would" delante del verbo con la excepción "should" o "could" donde "would" no es necesario ya que están expresados directamente en forma condicional.	Could	Podría
	Should	Debería
	Would go	Iría
	Would eat	Comería
I could go to run if the weather is nice Yo podría ir a correr si el clima está agradable	Would call	Llamaría
	Would wait	Esperaría
You should come to study only if you are ready for it Usted debería venir a estudiar sólo si usted está listo para ello	Would study	Estudiaría
	Would talk	Hablaría
I would go to visit you if you would be available for me Yo iría a visitarle si usted estuviera disponible para mí	Would take	Llevaría
	Would buy	Compraría
We would eat at your place if you would cook for all of us Nosotros comeríamos en su casa si ustedes cocinaran para todos nosotros	**Inglés Infinitivo**	**Español Infinitivo**
They would call you at noon if you could have an answer for them Ellos llamarían al mediodía si usted tuviera una respuesta para ellos	Can	Poder
I would take you to the airport if you are ready by 8 Yo le llevaría al aeropuerto si usted estuviera listo a las 8	Shall	Deber
	To go	Ir
You would be very happy if you could just try to lend a hand Usted se sentiría muy contento si simplemente tratara de dar una mano	To eat	Comer
	To call	Llamar
She would wait for them at noon if they are all showing up Ella esperaría por ellos al mediodía si todos ellos vienen	To wait	Esperar
	To talk	Hablar
They would preffer if you don't do anything for the moment Ellos preferirían que usted no haga nada por el momento	To study	Estudiar
	To buy	Comprar
He would try to finish tomorrow if he gets paid El trataría de terminar mañana si recibe el pago	To take	Llevar

El método de aprendizaje South Beach para inglés conversacional

Los 4 formatos en Fórmula

"LOS VERBOS INFINITIVOS" son la base de este curso (Empiezan con "To" en inglés y terminan con una "r" en español)

"The 4 Templates"

Gerundlo/ Gerund (Acción)
INGLÉS: To be + Verbo termina "ing"
ESPAÑOL: Estar + Verbo termina en o "iendo"
o "ando".
Cómo convertir un:
"Verbo Infinitivo" en inglés a Gerundio
To wait, elimine "To" y añada "ing" = waiting
"Verbo Infinitivo" en español a gerundio
esperar, elimine la "r" y añada "ando" =
Esperando Ejemplo: To Wait = Esperar (Verbo In
initivo)

I am waiting to eat
Yo estoy eperando para comer

Participio/Participle (Pasado Participio)
INGLÉS: To Have + Verbo en Participio
ESPAÑOL: Yo he   **Como convertir un**
verbo
                        Usted ha **Infinitivo a**
Participio: El ha   Elimine la "r" y añada
Ella ha   "ido" o "ado"
                Nosotros
hemos Ustedes han Ellos
han Eso/Esto ha
Ejemplo: To Wait = Esperar (Verbo Infinitivo)

I have been waiting for you
Yo he estado esperando por usted

Future/ Futuro
INGLÉS: Will + Verbo infinitivo
ESPAÑOL: Yo voy a
Usted va
a El va a
Ella va a
Nosotros vamos
a Ellos van a
Eso/esto va a
Ejemplo: To go = Ir, To eat = Comer (Verbos infinitvos)

I will go to eat later
Yo voy a ir a comer después

Conditional/ Condicional
INGLÉS: Could + Verbo infinitivo
          Should
          Would
ESPAÑOL: Verbo in initivo + "ia" o
"iera" Ejemplo: To go = Ir
                    To run = Correr (Verbos infinitvos)
I would go to run if you would come with me
Yo iría a correr si usted viniera conmigo

El método de aprendizaje South Beach para inglés conversacional

Los 4 formatos en Fórmula

A través de este método usted puede construir cualquier frase usando los "Verbos Infinitivos"
Escojamos un verbo : To Call (inglés) Llamar (español),(verbos infinitivos)

Gerundio/ Gerund (Acción)

Ejemplo:

Yo estoy llamándole

I am calling you

Gerundio en inglés es: To be + (ing)

Gerundio en español es: Estar + (ando), o (iendo). Verbo Infinitivo a Gerundio:
Llamar, eliminar la "r" = Llamando

Participio/Participle (Pasado Participio)

Ejemplo:

Yo he llamado al mediodía

I have called at noon

Participio en inglés es:
    To have + (verbo en participio pasado)
Participio en español es: Haber + (ido o ado)
Verbo infinitivo a Participio : Llamar eliminar "r" y añadir ido o ado = Llamado

Future/ Futuro

Ejemplo:

Yo voy a llamar

I will call

Futuro en inglés es : Will + (verbo infinitivo)
Futuro en español es: yo voy a + (verbo infintivo) Usted/el/ella/eso va a + (verbo infinitivo) Nosotros vamos a + (verbo infinitivo) Ustedes/ellos van a + (verbo infinitivo)

Conditional/Condicional

Ejemplo:

Yo llamaría más tarde

I would call later

Condicional en Inglés es: Would+(verbo infinitivo) Condicional en español es: Verbo infinitivo+ (ia) Verbo infinitivo a Condicional:
    Llamar+ ia = Llamaría

El método de aprendizaje South Beach para inglés conversacional

El truco de "did"

La manera más simple de hablar inglés en pasado es colocar/utilizar "did" antes del verbo.

(Actúa como filtro y convierte el verbo al tiempo pasado)

De esta manera (se) evita: tener que memorizar los verbos en pasado y siempre tener la duda de si está hablando correctamente

Ejemplos

Yo quiero comer **I want to eat**	Yo quise comer **I did want to eat**
Yo tengo que dormir **I have to sleep**	Yo tuve que dormir **I did have to sleep**
Usted habla con él **You talk to him**	Usted habló con él **You did talk to him**
Usted recibe correo **You get mail**	Usted recibió correo **You did get mail**

El método de aprendizaje South Beach para inglés conversacional

9avo. Paso de Aprendizaje

Los 11 verbos

La gramática inglesa en estos verbos es única y tiene diferencias con los demás verbos del idioma inglés

Practíquelos especialmente (la pronunciación)

LeCCIÓn No. 14

To be	Ser/estar	To have	Haber	Can	Poder
Could	Podría	Shall	Deber	Should	Debería
Will	Ir a	Must	Deber	Might	Poder
May	Podría	Would			

Estos 11 verbos tienen gramaticalmente características únicas que debemos tener presentes:

1) Si algún verbo sigue a estos verbos en una oración nunca habrá un "To" frente a él.

Ejemplos: En inglés, la mayor parte de las veces un "To" sigue al primer verbo: I have to go,I want to go, I like to go. Los 11 verbos son la excepción: I am going, I can go, I could go, I may go, I will go. Observe que no hay "To" en los segundos verbos.

2) Excepto To be y To have, la forma infinitiva en estos 11 verbos es también sin "To".

Ejemplo: Verbos Infinitivos en inglés comienzan con "To": To go, To want, pero 9 de esos 11 verbos no.

3) Cuando se hace una pregunta donde va alguno de esos 11 verbos no se usa "Do" o "Did" al comienzo de la pregunta, simplemente invertimos el orden del verbo y el pronombre (así es la única manera como lo hacen los hispanos).

Ejemplo:Normalmente se pregunta: Do I want?, Did I have?, pero con estos 11 verbos simplemente decimos: Am I?, Can I?

4) Cuando se niega con estos 11 verbos no se usan "Don´t" o "Didn´t, sino "not" después del verbo. Ejemplo: normalmente se niega I don´t want, I don´t have to, pero con estos verbos se niega. I am not coming, You can not go, You have not eaten.

5) Excepto To be y To have, estos verbos no tiene conjugaciones: I can, He can, I may, He may.

El método de aprendizaje South Beach para inglés conversacional

10vo. Paso de Aprendizaje

PREGUNTAS y NEGACIONES

Practíquelas, especialmente las conjugaciones y la pronunciación

LeCCIÓn No. 15

En inglés las preguntas son formuladas **insertando "do" (presente) o "did" (pasado) al principio de la frase**, (excepto los 11 verbos donde no se utiliza "do" o "did" sino que se coloca el verbo primero como en español)

Examples:

Usted quiere ir a comer
¿Quiere usted ir a comer?
(Do you want to go to eat?)

Usted tiene que venir
¿Tiene usted que venir?
(Do you have to come?)

Yo puedo ir a visitarla
¿Puedo yo ir a visitarla?
(Can I go to visit her?)

Ella debería llamarme
¿Debería ella llamarme?
(Should she call me?)

En inglés las negaciones son formuladas **insertando "do not" (presente) o "did not" (pasado) después del pronombre,** (excepto los 11 verbos donde no se utiliza "do" o "did" sino que sólo se coloca "not" después del verbo)

Examples:

Usted quiere ir a comer
Usted no quiere ir a comer
(You do not want to go to eat)

Usted tiene que venir
Usted no tiene que venir
(You don´t have to come)

Yo puedo ir a vistarla
Yo no puedo ir a visitarla
(I can not go to visit her)

Ella debería llamarme
Ella no debería llamarme
(She should not call me)

El método de aprendizaje South Beach para inglés conversacional

11vo. Paso de Aprendizaje

"THERE IS"

Practíquelo Especialmente

(la pronunciación)

LeCCIÓn No. 16

There is/ Hay (ah-ee)

There is: Hay (singular)

There are: Hay (plural)

There was: Hubo (singular)

There were: Hubo (plural)

There has been: Ha habido

There have been: Han habido

There will be: Va a haber

There would be: Habría o hubiera

There would have been: Hubieran habido

El método de aprendizaje South Beach para inglés conversacional

12vo. Paso de Aprendizaje

"Er-Est-Y"

Aprenda cómo estas terminaciones son utilizadas en inglés

Practíquelas, especialmente (la pronunciación)

LeCCIÓn No. 17 : Part E 1

Las terminaciones Er -Est –Y

Shorter	Más corto	Shortest	Lo más corto	
Better	Mejor	Best	Lo major	
Taller	Más alto	Tallest	Lo más alto	
Faster	Más rápido	Fastest	Lo más rápido	**Ejemplos:**
Quicker	Más rápido	Quickest	Lo más rápido	
Smaller	Más pequeño	Smallest	Lo más pequeño	Shorter than = Más corto que
Slower	Más despacio	Slowest	Lo mas despacio	Better than = Mejor que (*)
Hotter	Más caliente	Hottest	Lo más caliente	Taller than = Más alto que
Colder	Más frío	Coldest	Lo más frío	Faster than = Más rápido que
Dumber	Más tonto	Dumbest	Lo más tonto	
Fewer	Más poco	Fewest	Lo más poco	
Shorty	cortito o cortico	As___ as	Tan__como	
Tardy	retardado	More__than	Más__que	
Weepy	lloroso			

(*) Más y mejor are both superlatives , so they are never presented together

El método de aprendizaje South Beach para inglés conversacional

LeCCIÓn No. 17 : Part E 2

La Terminación **ER** cuando es aplicada a un verbo infinitivo la convierte en una persona

To drive	= manejar	Driver = conductor
To eat	= comer	Eater = comilón/glotón
To play	= jugar	Player = jugador
To run	= correr	Runner = corredor
To sleep	= dormir	Sleeper = dormilón
To write	= escribir	Writer = escritor
To read	= leer	Reader = lector
To pay	= pagar	Payer = pagador
To wash	= lavar	Washer = lavadora
To speak	= hablar	Speaker = hablador

13vo. Paso de Aprendizaje

EL VERBO "TO HAVE"

Aprenda las múltiples reglas gramaticales de este verbo

Practíquelas, especialmente las conjugaciones y (la pronunciación)

El método de aprendizaje South Beach para inglés conversacional

LeCCIÓn No. 18

El extraño caso del verbo To Have

En inglés dependiendo de su uso, existen tres usos y reglas gramaticales distintas para el verbo **"To have"** :

1) **Propiedad o posesión.** Ejemplos: I have a headache / Yo tengo un dolor de cabeza.

I have a son / Yo tengo un hijo.

2) **Deber o responsabilidad** . Ejemplos: I have to go / Yo me tengo que ir.

You have to come / Usted tiene que venir.

3) **Pasado Participio** . (como algo que ya ha pasado) Ejemplos: I have done it! / ¡Ya lo he hecho!
Pero cuando se trata de hacer una pregunta el verbo to have se complica. Cuando el verbo
to have se usa para propiedad o deber, se usan "Do or Did" :Do you have to go?/ I don't have to go.
Did you have to go? / Yes, I did have to go.

Pero cuando el verbo "to have" se usa como Participio Pasado no usamos "Do or Did".
Es el mismo verbo pero con reglas gramaticales totalmente distintas: Have you received a call? /
No I have not received any calls. Have you gotten any email?/ Yes I have gotten my mail today.

En español el verbo **"to have"** se expresa de la siguiente manera:

Tener	Tener que	Haber
Hold/ ownership	**Duty/ responsibility**	**(Already happened)**
I have a family	I have to go to eat	I have gone to eat early
Yo tengo una familia	Yo tengo que ir a comer	Yo he ido a comer temprano

El método de aprendizaje South Beach para inglés conversacional

14vo. Paso de Aprendizaje

La expresión "Acabo de"

El método de aprendizaje South Beach para inglés conversacional

LeCCIÓn No. 19: Part E 1

Inglés:

I have just	+ verbo en participio
You have just	+ verbo en participio
He has just	+ verbo en participio
She has just	+ verbo en participio
We have just	+ verbo en participio
You have just	+ verbo en participio
They have just	+ verbo en participio
It has just	+ verbo en participio

Español:

Yo me acabo de	+ verbo infinitivo
Usted se acaba de	+ verbo infinitivo
El se acaba de	+ verbo infinitivo
Ella se acaba de	+ verbo infinitivo
Nosotros nos acabamos de	+ verbo infinitivo
Ustedes se acaban de	+ verbo infinitivo
Ellos se acaban de	+ verbo infinitivo
Eso/Esto se acaba de	+ verbo infinitivo

Ejemplos:

(Yo) acabo de comer
I have just eaten
(Yo) Me acabo de levantar
I have just woken up
(El) acaba de llamar por teléfono
He has just phoned us
(Ellos) acaban de regresar de compras
They have just come back from shopping
(Ustedes) acaban de cometer un error
You have just committed (made) an error

(Usted) acaba de determinar su turno
You have just finished your shift
(Nosotros) Nos acabamos de ir
We have just left
(Ella) acaba de llevarle al colegio
She has just taken him to school
(Yo) Me acabo de recordar de la cita
I have just remembered the appointment
(Usted) Se acaba de perder la película
You have just missed the movie

El método de aprendizaje South Beach para inglés conversacional

Practiquemos

Practiquemos lo que hemos aprendido
(Usando el Verbo Infinitivo traduzca al inglés)

Ejemplos: <u>To Cook</u> (Verbo Infinitivo) Cocinar — Las 4 Plantillas/ Formato

Presente	Gerundio	Futuro	Pasado Participio	Condicional
I cook	I am cooking	I will cook	I have cooked	I would cook
Yo cocino	Yo estoy cocinando	Yo voy a cocinar	Yo he cocinado	Yo cocinaría
I will be cooking	I was cooking	I have to cook		I have been cooking
Yo voy a estar cocinando	Yo estaba cocinando	Yo tengo que cocinar		Yo he estado cocinando
I would have cooked	I did cook			
Yo hubiera cocinado	Yo cociné			

Ejemplos: <u>To Wait</u> (Verbo Infinitivo) Esperar — Las 4 Plantillas/ Formato

Presente	Gerundio	Futuro	Pasado Participio	Condicional
I wait	I am waiting	I will wait	I have waited	I would wait
Yo espero	Yo estoy esperando	Yo voy a esperar	Yo he esperado	Yo esperaría
I will be waiting	I was waiting	I have to wait		I have been waiting
Yo voy a estar esperando	Yo estaba esperando	Yo tengo que esperar		Yo he estado esperando
I would have waited	I did wait			
Yo hubiera esperado	Yo esperé			

El método de aprendizaje South Beach para inglés conversacional

Practiquemos

Practiquemos lo que hemos aprendido
(Usando el Verbo Infinitivo traduzca al inglés)

Ejemplos: Correr (Verbo Infinitivo) <u>To run</u>   **Las 4 Plantillas/ Formato**

Presente	Gerundio	Futuro	Pasado Participio	Condicional
Yo corro	Yo estoy corriendo	Yo voy a correr	Yo he corrido	Yo correría
Yo voy a estar corriendo	Yo estaba corriendo	Yo tengo que correr	Yo he estado corriendo	
Yo hubiera corrido	Yo corrí			

Ejemplos: Comer (Verbo Infinitivo) <u>To eat</u>   **Las 4 Plantillas/ Formato**

Presente	Gerundio	Futuro	Pasado Participio	Condicional
Yo como	Yo estoy comiendo	Yo voy a comer	Yo he comido	Yo comería
Yo voy a estar comiendo	Yo estaba comiendo	Yo tengo que comer	Yo he estado comiendo	
Yo hubiera comido	Yo comí			

El método de aprendizaje South Beach para inglés conversacional

Practiquemos

Practiquemos lo que hemos aprendido
(Usando el Verbo Infinitivo traduzca al inglés)

Ejemplos: Hablar (Verbo Infinitivo) To talk			Las 4 Plantillas/ Formato	
Presente Yo hablo	**Gerundio** Yo estoy hablando	**Futuro** Yo voy a hablar	**Pasado Participio** Yo he hablado	**Condicional** Yo hablaría
Yo voy a estar hablando	Yo estaba hablando	Yo tengo que hablar	Yo he estado hablando	
Yo hubiera hablado	Yo hablé			

Ejemplos: Llamar (Verbo Infinitivo) To call			Las 4 Plantillas/ Formato	
Presente Yo llamo	**Gerundio** Yo estoy llamando	**Futuro** Yo voy a llamar	**Pasado Participio** Yo he llamado	**Condicional** Yo llamaría
Yo voy a estar llamando	Yo estaba llamando	Yo tengo que llamar	Yo he estado llamando	
Yo hubiera llamado	Yo llamé			

El método de aprendizaje South Beach para inglés conversacional

Practiquemos

Practiquemos lo que hemos aprendido
(Usando el Verbo Infinitivo traduzca al inglés)

Ejemplos: Llevar (Verbo Infinitivo) To take — Las 4 Plantillas/ Formato

Presente	Gerundio	Futuro	Pasado Participio	Condicional
Yo llevo	Yo estoy llevando	Yo voy a llevar	Yo he llevado	Yo llevaría
Yo voy a estar llevando	Yo estaba llevando	Yo tengo que llevar	Yo he estado llevando	
Yo hubiera llevado	Yo llevé			

Ejemplos: Recibir (Verbo Infinitivo) To get — Las 4 Plantillas/ Formato

Presente	Gerundio	Futuro	Pasado Participio	Condicional
Yo recibo	Yo estoy recibiendo	Yo voy a recibir	Yo he recibido	Yo recibiría
Yo voy a estar recibiendo	Yo estaba recibiendo	Yo tengo que recibir	Yo he estado recibiendo	
Yo hubiera recibido	Yo recibí			

El método de aprendizaje South Beach para inglés conversacional

Practiquemos

Practiquemos lo que hemos aprendido
(Usando el Verbo Infinitivo traduzca al inglés)

Ejemplos: Pensar (Verbo Infinitivo) <u>To think</u>   **Las 4 Plantillas/ Formato**

Presente	Gerundio	Futuro	Pasado Participio	Condicional
Yo pienso	Yo estoy pensando	Yo voy a pensar	Yo he pensado	Yo pensaría
Yo voy a estar pensando	Yo estaba pensando	Yo tengo que pensar	Yo he estado pensando	
Yo hubiera pensado	Yo pensé			

Ejemplos: Estudiar (Verbo Infinitivo) <u>To study</u>   **Las 4 Plantillas/ Formato**

Presente	Gerundio	Futuro	Pasado Participio	Condicional
Yo estudio	Yo estoy estudiando	Yo voy a estudiar	Yo he estudiado	Yo estudiaría
Yo voy a estar estudiando	Yo estaba estudiando	Yo tengo que estudiar	Yo he estado estudiando	
Yo hubiera estudiado	Yo estudié			

El método de aprendizaje South Beach para inglés conversacional

Practiquemos

Practiquemos lo que hemos aprendido
(Usando el Verbo Infinitivo traduzca al inglés)

Ejemplos: Escribir (Verbo Infinitivo) To write			Las 4 Plantillas/ Formato	
Presente	**Gerundio**	**Futuro**	**Pasado Participio**	**Condicional**
Yo escribo	Yo estoy escribiendo	Yo voy a escribir	Yo he escrito	Yo escribiría
Yo voy a estar escribiendo	Yo estaba escribiendo	Yo tengo que escribir	Yo he estado escribiendo	
Yo hubiera escrito	Yo escribí			

Ejemplos: Leer (Verbo Infinitivo) To read			Las 4 Plantillas/ Formato	
Presente	**Gerundio**	**Futuro**	**Pasado Participio**	**Condicional**
Yo leo	Yo estoy leyendo	Yo voy a leer	Yo he leído	Yo leería
Yo voy a estar leyendo	Yo estaba leyendo	Yo tengo que leer	Yo he estado leyendo	
Yo hubiera leído	Yo leí			

El método de aprendizaje South Beach para inglés conversacional

Practiquemos

Practiquemos lo que hemos aprendido
(Usando el Verbo Infinitivo traduzca al inglés)

Ejemplos: Hacer (Verbo Infinitivo) To Do   Las 4 Plantillas/ Formato

Presente	Gerundio	Futuro	Pasado Participio	Condicional
Yo hago	Yo estoy haciendo	Yo voy a hacer	Yo he hecho	Yo haría
Yo voy a estar haciendo	Yo estaba haciendo	Yo tengo que hacer	Yo he estado haciendo	
Yo hubiera hecho	Yo hice			

Ejemplos: Trabajar (Verbo Infinitivo) To Work   Las 4 Plantillas/ Formato

Presente	Gerundio	Futuro	Pasado Participio	Condicional
Yo trabajo	Yo estoy trabajando	Yo voy a trabajar	Yo he trabajado	Yo trabajaría
Yo voy a estar trabajando	Yo estaba trabajando	Yo tengo que trabajar	Yo he estado trabajando	
Yo hubiera trabajado	Yo trabajé			

El método de aprendizaje South Beach para inglés conversacional

Practiquemos

Practiquemos lo que hemos aprendido "Negación"
(Usando el Verbo Infinitivo traduzca al inglés)

Ejemplos: <u>To Cook</u> (Verbo Infinitivo) Cocinar			Las 4 Plantillas/ Formato	
Presente	**Gerundio**	**Futuro**	**Pasado Participio**	**Condicional**
I don't cook	I am not cooking	I will not cook	I have not cooked	I would not cook
Yo no cocino	Yo no estoy cocinando	Yo no voy a cocinar	Yo no he cocinado	Yo no cocinaría

I will not be cooking	I was not cooking	I do not have to cook	I have not been cooking
Yo no voy a estar cocinando	Yo no estaba cocinando	Yo no tengo que cocinar	Yo no he estado cocinando

I would not have cooked	I did not cook
Yo no hubiera cocinado	Yo no cociné

Ejemplos: <u>To Wait</u> (Verbo Infinitivo) Esperar			Las 4 Plantillas/ Formato	
Presente	**Gerundio**	**Futuro**	**Pasado Participio**	**Condicional**
I don't wait	I am not waiting	I will not wait	I have not waited	I would not wait
Yo no espero	Yo no estoy esperando	Yo no voy a esperar	Yo no he esperado	Yo no esperaría

I will not be waiting	I was not waiting	I have not been waiting	I do not have to wait
Yo no voy a estar esperando	Yo no estaba esperando	Yo no he estado esperando	Yo no tengo que esperar

I would not have waited	I did not wait
Yo no hubiera esperado	Yo no esperé

El método de aprendizaje South Beach para inglés conversacional

Practiquemos

Practiquemos lo que hemos aprendido "Negación"
(Usando el Verbo Infinitivo traduzca al inglés)

Ejemplos: Correr (Verbo Infinitivo) <u>To Run</u>			Las 4 Plantillas/ Formato	
Presente	**Gerundio**	**Futuro**	**Pasado Participio**	**Condicional**
Yo no corro	Yo no estoy corriendo	Yo no voy a correr	Yo no he corrido	Yo no correría

Yo no voy a estar corriendo   Yo no estaba corriendo   Yo no tengo que correr   Yo no he estado corriendo

Yo no hubiera corrido   Yo no corrí

Ejemplos: Comer (Verbo Infinitivo) <u>To Eat</u>			Las 4 Plantillas/ Formato	
Presente	**Gerundio**	**Futuro**	**Pasado Participio**	**Condicional**
Yo no como	Yo no estoy comiendo	Yo no voy a comer	Yo no he comido	Yo no comería

Yo no voy a estar comiendo   Yo no estaba comiendo   Yo no tengo que comer   Yo no he estado comiendo

Yo no hubiera comido   Yo no comí

El método de aprendizaje South Beach para inglés conversacional

Practiquemos

Practiquemos lo que hemos aprendido "Negación"
(Usando el Verbo Infinitivo traduzca al inglés)

Ejemplos: Hablar (Verbo Infinitivo) To Talk			Las 4 Plantillas/ Formato	
Presente Yo no hablo	**Gerundio** Yo no estoy hablando	**Futuro** Yo no voy a hablar	**Pasado Participio** Yo no he hablado	**Condicional** Yo no hablaría

Yo no voy a estar hablando   Yo no estaba hablando   Yo no tengo que hablar Yo no he estado hablando

Yo no hubiera hablado   Yo no hablé

Ejemplos: Llamar (Verbo Infinitivo) To Call			Las 4 Plantillas/ Formato	
Presente Yo no llamo	**Gerundio** Yo no estoy llamando	**Futuro** Yo no voy a llamar	**Pasado Participio** Yo no he llamado	**Condicional** Yo no llamaría

Yo no voy a estar llamando   Yo no estaba llamando   Yo no tengo que llamar   Yo no he estado llamando

Yo no hubiera llamado   Yo no llamé

Practiquemos

Practiquemos lo que hemos aprendido "Negación"
(Usando el Verbo Infinitivo traduzca al inglés)

Ejemplos: Llevar (Verbo Infinitivo) <u>To Take</u>			Las 4 Plantillas/ Formato	
Presente	**Gerundio**	**Futuro**	**Pasado Participio**	**Condicional**
Yo no llevo	Yo no estoy llevando	Yo no voy a llevar	Yo no he llevado	Yo no llevaría

Yo no voy a estar llevando   Yo no estaba llevando   Yo no tengo que llevar   Yo no he estado llevando

Yo no hubiera llevado   Yo no llevé

Ejemplos: Recibir (Verbo Infinitivo) <u>To Get</u>			Las 4 Plantillas/ Formato	
Presente	**Gerundio**	**Futuro**	**Pasado Participio**	**Condicional**
Yo no recibo	Yo no estoy recibiendo	Yo no voy a recibir	Yo no he recibido	Yo no recibiría

Yo no voy a estar recibiendo Yo no estaba recibiendo Yo no tengo que recibir Yo no he estado recibiendo

Yo no hubiera recibido   Yo no recibí

El método de aprendizaje South Beach para inglés conversacional

Practiquemos

Practiquemos lo que hemos aprendido "Negación"
(Usando el Verbo Infinitivo traduzca al inglés)

Ejemplos: Pensar (Verbo Infinitivo) To Think			Las 4 Plantillas/ Formato	
Presente	**Gerundio**	**Futuro**	**Pasado Participio**	**Condicional**
Yo no pienso	Yo no estoy pensando	Yo no voy a pensar	Yo no he pensado	Yo no pensaría

Yo no voy a estar pensando Yo no estaba pensando Yo no tengo que pensar Yo no he estado pensando

Yo no hubiera pensado   Yo no pensé

Ejemplos: Estudiar (Verbo Infinitivo) To Study			Las 4 Plantillas/ Formato	
Presente	**Gerundio**	**Futuro**	**Pasado Participio**	**Condicional**
Yo no estudio	Yo no estoy estudiando	Yo no voy a estudiar	Yo no he estudiado	Yo no estudiaría

Yo no voy a estar estudiando   Yo no estaba estudiando   Yo no tengo que estudiar

Yo no hubiera estudiado   Yo no estudié   Yo no he estado estudiando

Practiquemos

Practiquemos lo que hemos aprendido "Negación"
(Usando el Verbo Infinitivo traduzca al inglés)

Ejemplos: Escribir (Verbo Infinitivo) <u>To Write</u>   Las 4 Plantillas/ Formato

Presente	Gerundio	Futuro	Pasado Participio	Condicional
Yo no escribo	Yo no estoy escribiendo	Yo no voy a escribir	Yo no he escrito	Yo no escribiría
Yo no voy a estar escribiendo	Yo no estaba escribiendo	Yo no tengo que escribir		
Yo no hubiera escrito	Yo no escribí			Yo no he estado escribiendo

Ejemplos: Leer (Verbo Infinitivo) <u>To Read</u>   Las 4 Plantillas/ Formato

Presente	Gerundio	Futuro	Pasado Participio	Condicional
Yo no leo	Yo no estoy leyendo	Yo no voy a leer	Yo no he leído	Yo no leería
Yo no voy a estar leyendo	Yo no estaba leyendo	Yo no tengo que leer	Yo no he estado leyendo	
Yo no hubiera leído	Yo no leí			

Practiquemos

Practiquemos lo que hemos aprendido "Negación"
(Usando el Verbo Infinitivo traduzca al inglés)

Ejemplos: Hacer (Verbo Infinitivo) To Do			Las 4 Plantillas/ Formato	
Presente	**Gerundio**	**Futuro**	**Pasado Participio**	**Condicional**
Yo no hago	Yo no estoy haciendo	Yo no voy a hacer	Yo no he hecho	Yo no haría
Yo no voy a estar haciendo	Yo no estaba haciendo	Yo no tengo que hacer	Yo no he estado haciendo	
Yo no hubiera hecho	Yo no hice			

Ejemplos: Trabajar (Verbo Infinitivo) To Work			Las 4 Plantillas/ Formato	
Presente	**Gerundio**	**Futuro**	**Pasado Participio**	**Condicional**
Yo no trabajo	Yo no estoy trabajando	Yo no voy a trabajar	Yo no he trabajado	Yo no trabajaría
Yo no voy a estar trabajando	Yo no estaba trabajando	Yo no tengo que trabajar		
Yo no hubiera trabajado	Yo no trabajé		Yo no he estado trabajando	

El método de aprendizaje South Beach para inglés conversacional

Practiquemos

Practiquemos lo que hemos aprendido "Preguntas"
(Usando el Verbo Infinitivo traduzca al inglés)

Ejemplos: <u>To Cook</u> (Verbo Infinitivo) Cocinar　　　　　　　**Las 4 Plantillas/ Formato**

Presente	**Gerundio**	**Futuro**	**Pasado Participio**	**Condicional**
Do I cook?	Am I cooking?	Will I cook?	Have I cooked?	Would I cook?
¿Cocino yo?	¿Estoy yo cocinando?	¿Voy a cocinar yo?	¿He yo cocinado?	¿Cocinaría yo?

Will I be cooking?	Was I cooking?	Do I have to cook?	Have I been cooking?
¿Voy a estar cocinando yo?	¿Estaba cocinando yo?	¿Tengo yo que cocinar?	¿He estado cocinando yo?
Would I have cooked?	Did I cook?		
¿Hubiera yo cocinado?	¿Cociné Yo?		

Ejemplos: <u>To Wait</u> (Verbo Infinitivo) Esperar　　　　　　　**Las 4 Plantillas/ Formato**

Presente	**Gerundio**	**Futuro**	**Pasado Participio**	**Condicional**
Do I wait?	Am I waiting?	Will I wait?	Have I waited?	Would I wait?
¿Espero yo?	¿Estoy yo esperando?	¿Voy yo a esperar?	¿He yo esperado?	¿Esperaría yo?

Will I be waiting?	Was I waiting?	Do I have to wait?	Have I been waiting?
¿Voy a estar esperando yo?	¿Estaba esperando yo?	¿Tengo que esperar yo?	¿He estado esperando yo?
Would I have waited?	Did I wait?		
¿Hubiera esperado yo?	¿Esperé yo?		

El método de aprendizaje South Beach para inglés conversacional

Practiquemos

Practiquemos lo que hemos aprendido "Preguntas"
(Usando el Verbo Infinitivo traduzca al inglés)

Ejemplos: Correr (Verbo Infinitivo) To Run			Las 4 Plantillas/ Formato	
Presente ¿Corro yo?	**Gerundio** ¿Estoy corriendo yo?	**Futuro** ¿Voy a correr yo?	**Pasado Participio** ¿He corrido yo?	**Condicional** ¿Correría yo?

¿Voy a estar corriendo yo?   ¿Estaba corriendo yo?   ¿Tengo que correr yo?   ¿He estado corriendo yo?

¿Hubiera corrido yo?   ¿Corrí yo?

Ejemplos: Comer (Verbo Infinitivo) To eat			Las 4 Plantillas/ Formato	
Presente ¿Como yo?	**Gerundio** ¿Estoy comiendo yo?	**Futuro** ¿Voy a comer yo?	**Pasado Participio** ¿He comido yo?	**Condicional** ¿Comería yo?

¿Voy a estar comiendo yo?   ¿Estaba comiendo yo?   ¿Tengo que comer yo?   ¿He estado comiendo yo?

¿Hubiera comido yo?   ¿Comí yo?

El método de aprendizaje South Beach para inglés conversacional

Practiquemos

Practiquemos lo que hemos aprendido "Preguntas"
(Usando el Verbo Infinitivo traduzca al inglés)

Ejemplos: Hablar (Verbo Infinitivo) To talk			Las 4 Plantillas/ Formato	
Presente ¿Hablo yo?	**Gerundio** ¿Estoy hablando yo?	**Futuro** ¿Voy a hablar yo?	**Pasado Participio** ¿He hablado yo?	**Condicional** ¿Hablaría yo?

¿Voy a estar hablando yo?   ¿Estaba hablando yo?   ¿Tengo que hablar yo? ¿He estado hablando yo?

¿Hubiera hablado yo?   ¿Hablé yo?

Ejemplos: Llamar (Verbo Infinitivo) To call			Las 4 Plantillas/ Formato	
Presente ¿Llamo yo?	**Gerundio** ¿Estoy llamando yo?	**Futuro** ¿Voy a llamar yo?	**Pasado Participio** ¿He llamado yo?	**Condicional** ¿Llamaría yo?

¿Voy a estar llamando yo?   ¿Estaba llamando yo? ¿Tengo que llamar yo?   ¿He estado llamando yo?

¿Hubiera llamado yo?   ¿Llamé yo?

Practiquemos

Practiquemos lo que hemos aprendido "Preguntas"
(Usando el Verbo Infinitivo traduzca al inglés)

Ejemplos: Llevar (Verbo Infinitivo) To take			Las 4 Plantillas/ Formato	
Presente	**Gerundio**	**Futuro**	**Pasado Participio**	**Condicional**
¿Llevo yo?	¿Estoy llevando yo?	¿Voy a llevar yo?	¿He llevado yo?	¿Llevaría yo?

¿Voy a estar llevando yo?   ¿Estaba llevando yo?   ¿Tengo que llevar yo? ¿He estado llevando yo?

¿Hubiera llevado yo?   ¿Llevé yo?

Ejemplos: Recibir (Verbo Infinitivo) To get			Las 4 Plantillas/ Formato	
Presente	**Gerundio**	**Futuro**	**Pasado Participio**	**Condicional**
¿Recibo yo?	¿Estoy recibiendo yo?	¿Voy a recibir yo?	¿He recibido yo?	¿Recibiría yo?

¿Voy a estar recibiendo yo? ¿Estaba recibiendo yo?   ¿Tengo que recibir yo? ¿He estado recibiendo yo?

¿Hubiera recibido yo?   ¿Recibí yo?

Practiquemos

Practiquemos lo que hemos aprendido "Preguntas"
(Usando el Verbo Infinitivo traduzca al inglés)

Ejemplos: Pensar (Verbo Infinitivo) <u>To think</u>			Las 4 Plantillas/ Formato	
Presente ¿Pienso yo?	**Gerundio** ¿Estoy pensando yo?	**Futuro** ¿Voy a pensar yo?	**Pasado Participio** ¿He pensado yo?	**Condicional** ¿Pensaría yo?

¿Voy a estar pensando yo? ¿Estaba pensando yo? ¿Tengo que pensar yo? ¿He estado pensando yo?

¿Hubiera pensado yo?   ¿Pensé yo?

Ejemplos: Estudiar (Verbo Infinitivo) <u>To study</u>			Las 4 Plantillas/ Formato	
Presente ¿Estudio yo?	**Gerundio** ¿Estoy estudiando yo?	**Futuro** ¿Voy a estudiar yo?	**Pasado Participio** ¿He estudiado yo?	**Condicional** ¿Estudiaría yo?

¿Voy a estar estudiando yo? ¿Estaba estudiando yo? ¿Tengo que estudiar yo? ¿He estado estudiando yo?

¿Hubiera estudiado yo?   ¿Estudié yo?

El método de aprendizaje South Beach para inglés conversacional

Practiquemos

Practiquemos lo que hemos aprendido "Preguntas"
(Usando el Verbo Infinitivo traduzca al inglés)

Ejemplos: Escribir (Verbo Infinitivo) To write   **Las 4 Plantillas/ Formato**

Presente	Gerundio	Futuro	Pasado Participio	Condicional
¿Escribo yo?	¿Estoy escribiendo yo?	¿Voy a escribir yo?	¿He escrito yo?	¿Escribiría yo?

¿Voy a estar escribiendo yo? ¿Estaba escribiendo yo? ¿Tengo que escribir yo? ¿He estado escribiendo yo?

¿Hubiera escrito yo?   ¿Escribí yo?

Ejemplos: Leer (Verbo Infinitivo) To read   **Las 4 Plantillas/ Formato**

Presente	Gerundio	Futuro	Pasado Participio	Condicional
¿Leo yo?	¿Estoy leyendo yo?	¿Voy a leer yo?	¿He leído yo?	¿Leería yo?

¿Voy a estar leyendo yo?   ¿Estaba leyendo yo?   ¿Tengo que leer yo?   ¿He estado leyendo yo?

¿Hubiera leído yo?   ¿Leí yo?

El método de aprendizaje South Beach para inglés conversacional

Practiquemos

Practiquemos lo que hemos aprendido "Preguntas"
(Usando el Verbo Infinitivo traduzca al inglés)

Ejemplos: Hacer (Verbo Infinitivo) <u>To do</u>			Las 4 Plantillas/ Formato	
Presente ¿Hago yo?	Gerundio ¿Estoy haciendo yo?	Futuro ¿Voy a hacer yo?	**Pasado Participio** ¿He hecho yo?	Condicional ¿Haría yo?

¿Voy a estar haciendo yo? ¿Estaba haciendo yo? ¿Tengo que hacer yo? ¿He estado haciendo yo?

¿Hubiera hecho yo?   ¿Hice yo?

Ejemplos: Trabajar (Verbo Infinitivo) <u>To work</u>			Las 4 Plantillas/ Formato	
Presente ¿Trabajo yo?	Gerundio ¿Estoy trabajando yo?	Futuro ¿Voy a trabajar yo?	**Pasado Participio** ¿He trabajado yo?	Condicional ¿Trabajaría yo?

¿Voy a estar trabajando yo? ¿Estaba trabajando yo? ¿Tengo que trabajar yo? ¿He estado trabajando yo?

¿Hubiera trabajado yo?   ¿Trabajé yo?

El método de aprendizaje South Beach para inglés conversacional

Vocabulario en Inglés

A

A: To
Abril: April
A esta hora: At this time
A las: At (Hora)
A menos que: Unless
A menudo: Often
A pesar de: Despite
A propósito: By the way
A punto de: Almost
A qué distancia: How far
A qué hora: At what time
A quién: Whom
A través: Through
A través de lo cual: Whereby
Abajo: Under
Abierto: Open
Abrigo: Coat
Acerca de: About
Adentro: Inside
Adonde: Where to
Aduana: Customs
Afuera: Outside
Agradable: Nice, pleasant
Agua: Water
Ahora: Now
Ahora mismo: Right now
Aerolínea: Airline
Aire: Air

Aire: Air
Avión: Airplane
Algo: Something, somewhat
Alguien: Someone, somebody
Alguno: Some
Al lado: Next to
Allá: There
Almacén: Warehouse
Alto: Tall
Almacén: Store
Amable: Kind
Amarillo: Yellow
Ambos: Both
Amistoso: Friendly
Año: Year
Ancho: Wide
Antes: Before
Apenado: Embarrased
Apenas: Barely
Aquellos: Those
Aquí: Here
Arriba: Up, over
Arriba de: Above of
Arroz: Rice
Asado: Roasted
Aturdido: Dizzy
Aun cuando: Even though
Aunque: Nevertheless

Autobus: Bus
Automovil: Automobile
Aviso: Notice
Ayer: Yesterday
Ayuda: Help, id   Azafata:
Stewardess Azúcar:
Sugar
A propósito: By the way
A pesar de: In spite of
Ajo: Garlic

B

Baile: Dance
Bajo: Low, short
Banco: Bank
Bandera: Flag
Baño: Restroom
Barato: Cheap
Barco: Boat, ship
Básico: Basic
Bastante: Plenty, enough
Bebé: Baby
Bicicleta: Bicycle
Bien: Well, fine
Bien sea: Whether
Bocadillo: Snack
Bolsa: Bag
Bolsillo: Pocket

El método de aprendizaje South Beach para inglés conversacional

Vocabulario en Inglés

Bulto: Bulk
Bota: Boot
Botella: Bottle
Botón: Button
Bueno: Good
Billetera: Wallet

C

Cada: Each, every
Caliente: Hot
Carente de: Lacking of
Casi: Almost,
Cautela: Caution
Ceder el paso: Yield
Cerca: Near
Cierto: Certain, true
Clase: Kind, class
Colapso: Collapse
Cómo: How
Completo: Complete
Con: With
Conmigo: With me
Cosa: Thing
Considerando que: Whereas
Contigo: With You
Cuál: Which, What
Cualquiera: Anyone

Cuando: When
Cuando sea: Whenever
Cuánto: How much
Cuidado: Careful

D

Dama: Lady
De: Of, from
De buena gana: Willingly
De cualquier manera: Anyway
De guardia: On call
De nuevo: Again
De otra manera; Otherwise
De quien: Whose
Debajo: Underneath, under
Delgado: Skinny
Demasiado: Enough
Dentista: Dentist
Dentro: Inside
Deportes: Sports
Derecho(a): Right
Desafortunadamente: Unfortunately
Desagradable: Unpleasant
Derecho(a): Right
Descuento: Discount
Desierto: Desert
Desfile: Parade
Dentro de: Within

Despacio: Slow
Después: After, afterwards
Detrás de: Behind
Desviación: Detour, deviation
Día: Day
Diario: Daily
Diez: Ten
Difícil: Difficult
Diciembre: December
Diccionario: Dictionary
Dinero: Money
Dirección: Address
Disponible: Available
Divertido: Fun, amusing
Dividido por: Enter, Divided by
Doce: Twelve
Dolor: Ache, pain
Dónde: Where
Donde se encuentre: Wherever
Docena: Dozen
Ducha: Shower

E

En particular: In particular En proceso: In process
En seguida: Right away
En vez de: Instead of

El método de aprendizaje South Beach para inglés conversacional

Vocabulario en Inglés

Entre: Between
Es necesario: It's necessary
Esta noche: Tonight
Específico: Specific
Esto(a): It, this
Estos: These
Extraño: Strange
Estrecho: Narrow
Empujar: Push
En: On, in
En algún lugar: Someplace
En buena salud: In good health
En caso de: In case of
En contra de: Against
En este momento: In this moment
En frente de: In front of
En la: In the
En orden de: In order to

F

Fácilmente: Easily
Factible: Possible
Falla: Fault
Familia: Family
Farmacia: Pharmacy
Febrero: February
Feria: Fair
Ferrocarril: Train

Fiebre: Fever
Fiesta: Party
Fino: Fine
Frito: Fried
Fruta: Fruit
Fuego: Fire

G

Gas: Gas
Gasolina: Gasoline

Grande: Big
Grueso: Thick
Goteo: Drip, leak
Gafas: Glasses
Gracias: Thank You
Gratis: Free
Gris: Gray
Gente: People
Gerente: Manager
Guante: Glove
Guía: Guide
Guisantes: Green peas

H

Habrá: There will be
Hay: There is or are
Hombres: Men

Horno: Oven
Hace: Ago
Hecho en: Made in
Hora: Hour
Huevo: Egg
Hacia: To, towards
Helado: Ice cream
Horario: Time table
Halar: Pull
Hombre: Man
Generalmente: Generally
Horneado: Baked
Hasta luego: See you later
Hubo: There were or was
Habrían estado: There would have been
Habrían sido: There would have been
Ha habido: There have had
Habrían habido: There would have had
Han estado: There have been
Han sido: There have been

I

Ida y vuelta: Round trip
Iglesia: Church
Imposible: Impossible
Improbable: Improbable
Incluido: Included
Inmediatamente: Immediately
Inodoro: Toilet

El método de aprendizaje South Beach para inglés conversacional

Vocabulario en Inglés

Insecto: Insect
Izquierda: Left

J
Jabón: Soap
Jefe: Boss
Joyas: Jewelry
Juego: Game
Jugo: Juice
Junio: June
Juntos: Together
Justo: Just, Fair

L
Llave: Key
Lluvia: Rain
Loco: Crazy
Lúcido: Lucid
Luego: After
Lunes: Monday
Lado: Side
Ladron: Thief
Largo: Long
Lavabo: Sink
Lavamanos: Sink
Laxante: Laxative
Leche: Milk
Lechuga: Lettuce
Legal: Legal
Legumbres: Legumes
Lejos: Far
Lentes: Glasses
Lento: Slow
Libre: Free
Limón: Lemon
Limonada: Lemonade
Listo: Ready, smart (male)
Lista: List, smart (female)

M
Maleta: Suitcase
Mañana: Tomorrow
Mantener: Keep, maintain
Mantequilla: Butter
Manzana: Apple
Máquina: Machine
Marido: Husband
Marrón: Brown
Más allá: Beyond, further
Menos: Less, minus
Media: Half
Medianoche: Midnight
Medio: Middle
Mediodía: Mid-day, noon
Menú: Menu
Mensaje: Message
Menos: Less, minus
Mermelada: Marmelade
Mes: Month
Mesonero: Waiter
Mientras que: While
Mucho: A lot, much
Mientras: While
Muchos: Many

N
Naranja: Orange
Nave: Ship, boat
Necesariamente: Necessarily
Necesario: Necesarily, needful
Necesitado: Needed
Ninguno: None
No: Not, No
Nuevo: New
Nuevamente: Again
Nunca: Never

O
O: Or
Objetos de valor: Valuables
Obras: Works
Obvio: Obvious
Ocupado: Busy

El método de aprendizaje South Beach para inglés conversacional

Vocabulario en Inglés

Octubre: October
Ojo: Eye
Once: Eleven
Oscuro: Dark Otoño:
Autum, fall Otro:
Other, another

P

Placer: Pleasure
Plancha: Iron
Poco: Few, bit
Por consiguiente: Therefore
Por costumbre: In the habit
Por la razón: For the reason
Por lo tanto: Hence
Por qué: Why
Pregunta: Question
Presentar: Introduce
Primavera: Spring
Privado: Private
Probablemente: Probably
Problema: Problem
Profundamente: Profoundly
Pronto: Soon
Próximo: Next
Poco: A little
Policía: Police
Por ciento: Percent

Portero: Porter
Puede Ser: It can be
Punto: Point
Panadería: Bakery
Pañales: Diapers
Papá: Father
Para: For
Pare: Stop
Pareciera: Seemingly
Parece: Seems like
Parque: Park
Pasaje: Ticket
Papas: Potatoes
Papel higiénico: Toilet paper
Paraguas: Umbrella
Pasaporte: Passport
Payment: Pago
Película: Movie
Pequeño: Small, Little
Por día: Per day
Por supuesto: Of course
Postre: Dessert
Perdóneme: Excuse me
Pero: But
Pesado: Heavy
Pasajero: Passenger

Q

Querido: Dear
Queso: Cheese
Quizás: Maybe
Que: What, that

R

Radiador: Radiator
Rápido: Fast
Rebaja: Rebate
Rebajas: Bargains
Regalo: Gift
Relativo: Relative
Reloj: Watch
Regularmente: Regularly
Repita: Repeat
Ridículo: Ridicule
Riña: Fight
Robo: Theft Ropa:
Clothes
Responsable: Responsible
Ruido: Noise
Rutina: Routine
Ruptura: Rupture

S

Sabiduría: Wisdom
Sabor: Taste

El método de aprendizaje South Beach para inglés conversacional

Vocabulario en Inglés

Sabroso: Tasty
Sacar: To pull
Sacrificar: Sacrifice
Sagrado: Sacred
Saltar: To jump
Secreto: Secret
Serio: Serious
Servicio: Service
Silbar: To whistle
Silencio: Silence
Sistema: System
Sociedad: Society
Soleado: Sunny
Soledad: Loneliness
Solidez: Strength
Sordo: Deaf
Sorpresa: Surprise
Sublime: Sublime
Suspiro: Sigh
Sustituir: Substitute
Susto: Fright
Susurro: Whisper

T

Tachar: To scratch
Tacaño: Cheap
Taller: Workshop
Tambor: Drum
Tangente: Tangent
Taxista: Taxi driver
Techo: Roof
Teja: Roof tile
Tema: Theme
Temor: Fear
Temprano: Early
Tendencia: Tendency
Terreno: Plot of land
Tesoro: Treasure
Tiempo: Time
Timbrar: Ring the bell
Timbre: Ring
Tiza: Chalk
Tristeza: Sadness
Todopoderoso: Almighty
Tonto: Fool
Tos: Cough
Tribuna: Tribune
Tumultuoso: Tumultous, crowded
Tunel: Tunnel
Turismo: Tourism

U

Último: Last
Urgencia: Urgency
Urgente: Urgent
Utilidad: Usefulness

Usual: Usual
Usurero: Usurer
Usurpar: To usurp
Usuario: User
Urbanista: City planner
Universo: Universe
Universidad: University

V

Vacaciones: Vacations
Vacante: Vacant
Variedad: Variety
Valor: Valor
Vanidad: Vanity
Vehículo: Vehicle
Velero: Sailboat
Verdad: Truth
Versatil: Versatile
Vicioso: Vicious
Victorioso: Victorious
Vida: Life
Viejo: Old
Víspera: Eve
Vitamina: Vitamin
Virilidad: Virility
Voraz: Voracious

W X

Y

Yacimiento: Deposit
Yanqui: Yankee
Yarda: Yard
Yerba: Grass

Z

Zancadilla: Trip
Zángano: Lazy
Zapato: Shoe
Zapatero: Shoe maker
Zona: Zone
Zumbido: Buzz
Zumo: Juice
Zorro: Fox

El método de aprendizaje South Beach para inglés conversacional

Verbos esenciales en el idioma inglés

A   Abrir: To Open

	Presente	Pasado	Futuro	Participio	Condicional
I	Open	Opened	Will Open	Have Opened	Would Open
You	Open	Opened	Will Open	Have Opened	Would Open
He	Opens	Opened	Will Open	Has Opened	Would Open
She	Opens	Opened	Will Open	Has Opened	Would Open
We	Open	Opened	Will Open	Have Opened	Would Open
You	Open	Opened	Will Open	Have Opened	Would Open
They	Open	Opened	Will Open	Have Opened	Would Open
It	Opens	Opened	Will Open	Has Opened	Would Open

Abrazar: To Hug

	Presente	Pasado	Futuro	Participio	Condicional
I	Hug	Hugged	Will Hug	Have Hugged	Would Hug
You	Hug	Hugged	Will Hug	Have Hugged	Would Hug
He	Hugs	Hugged	Will Hug	Has Hugged	Would Hug
She	Hugs	Hugged	Will Hug	Has Hugged	Would Hug
We	Hug	Hugged	Will Hug	Have Hugged	Would Hug
You	Hug	Hugged	Will Hug	Have Hugged	Would Hug
They	Hug	Hugged	Will Hug	Have Hugged	Would Hug
It	Hugs	Hugged	Will Hug	Has Hugged	Would Hug

Acceptar: To Accept

	Presente	Pasado	Futuro	Participio	Condicional
I	Accept	Accepted	Will Accept	Have Accepted	Would Accept
You	Accept	Accepted	Will Accept	Have Accepted	Would Accept
He	Accepts	Accepted	Will Accept	Has Accepted	Would Accept
She	Accepts	Accepted	Will Accept	Has Accepted	Would Accept
We	Accept	Accepted	Will Accept	Have Accepted	Would Accept
You	Accept	Accepted	Will Accept	Have Accepted	Would Accept
They	Accept	Accepted	Will Accept	Have Accepted	Would Accept
It	Accepts	Accepted	Will Accept	Has Accepted	Would Accept

El método de aprendizaje South Beach para inglés conversacional

Verbos esenciales en el idioma inglés

A   Acertar: To Be Right

	Presente	Pasado	Futuro	Participio	Condicional
I	Am right	was right	Will be right	Have been right	Would be right
You	Are right	were right	Will be right	Have been right	Would be right
He	Is right	was right	Will be right	Has been right	Would be right
She	Is right	was right	Will be right	Has been right	Would be right
We	Are right	were right	Will be right	Have been right	Would be right
You	Are right	were right	Will be right	Have been right	Would be right
They	Are right	were right	Will be right	Have been right	Would be right
It	Is right	was right	Will be right	Has been right	Would be right

Adquirir: To Acquire

	Presente	Pasado	Futuro	Participio	Condicional
I	acquire	acquired	Will acquire	Have acquired	Would acquire
You	acquire	acquired	Will acquire	Have acquired	Would acquire
He	acquires	acquired	Will acquire	Has acquired	Would acquire
She	acquires	acquired	Will acquire	Has acquired	Would acquire
We	acquire	acquired	Will acquire	Have acquired	Would acquire
You	acquire	acquired	Will acquire	Have acquired	Would acquire
They	acquire	acquired	Will acquire	Have acquired	Would acquire
It	acquires	acquired	Will acquire	Has acquired	Would acquire

Agradecer: To Thank

	Presente	Pasado	Futuro	Participio	Condicional
I	thank	thanked	Will thank	Have thanked	Would thank
You	thank	thanked	Will thank	Have thanked	Would thank
He	thanks	thanked	Will thank	Has thanked	Would thank
She	thanks	thanked	Will thank	Has thanked	Would thank
We	thank	thanked	Will thank	Have thanked	Would thank
You	thank	thanked	Will thank	Have thanked	Would thank
They	thank	thanked	Will thank	Have thanked	Would thank
It	thanks	thanked	Will thank	Has thanked	Would thank

El método de aprendizaje South Beach para inglés conversacional

Verbos esenciales en el idioma inglés

Anunciar: To Announce

	Presente	Pasado	Futuro	Participio	Condicional
I	Announce	Announced	Will Announce	Have Announced	Would Announce
You	Announce	Announced	Will Announce	Have Announced	Would Announce
He	Announces	Announced	Will Announce	Has Announced	Would Announce
She	Announces	Announced	Will Announce	Has Announced	Would Announce
We	Announce	Announced	Will Announce	Have Announced	Would Announce
You	Announce	Announced	Will Announce	Have Announced	Would Announce
They	Announce	Announced	Will Announce	Have Announced	Would Announce
It	Announces	Announced	Will Announce	Has Announced	Would Announce

Amar: To Love

	Presente	Pasado	Futuro	Participio	Condicional
I	Love	Loved	Will Love	Have Loved	Would Love
You	Love	Loved	Will Love	Have Loved	Would Love
He	Loves	Loved	Will Love	Has Loved	Would Love
She	Loves	Loved	Will Love	Has Loved	Would Love
We	Love	Loved	Will Love	Have Loved	Would Love
You	Love	Loved	Will Love	Have Loved	Would Love
They	Love	Loved	Will Love	Have Loved	Would Love
It	Loves	Loved	Will Love	Has Loved	Would Love

Aprender: To Learn

	Presente	Pasado	Futuro	Participio	Condicional
I	Learn	Learned	Will Learn	Have Learned	Would Learn
You	Learn	Learned	Will Learn	Have Learned	Would Learn
He	Learns	Learned	Will Learn	Has Learned	Would Learn
She	Learns	Learned	Will Learn	Has Learned	Would Learn
We	Learn	Learned	Will Learn	Have Learned	Would Learn
You	Learn	Learned	Will Learn	Have Learned	Would Learn
They	Learn	Learned	Will Learn	Have Learned	Would Learn
It	Learns	Learned	Will Learn	Has Learned	Would Learn

Verbos esenciales en el idioma inglés

Ayudar : To Help

	Presente	Pasado	Futuro	Participio	Condicional
I	help	helped	Will help	Have helped	Would help
You	help	helped	Will help	Have helped	Would help
He	helps	helped	Will help	Has helped	Would help
She	helps	helped	Will help	Has helped	Would help
We	help	helped	Will help	Have helped	Would help
You	help	helped	Will help	Have helped	Would help
They	help	helped	Will help	Have helped	Would help
It	helps	helped	Will help	Has helped	Would help

Bailar: To Dance

	Presente	Pasado	Futuro	Participio	Condicional
I	dance	danced	Will dance	Have danced	Would dance
You	dance	danced	Will dance	Have danced	Would dance
He	dances	danced	Will dance	Has danced	Would dance
She	dances	danced	Will dance	Has danced	Would dance
We	dance	danced	Will dance	Have danced	Would dance
You	dance	danced	Will dance	Have danced	Would dance
They	dance	danced	Will dance	Have danced	Would dance
It	dances	danced	Will dance	Has danced	Would dance

Beber: To Drink

	Presente	Pasado	Futuro	Participio	Condicional
I	drink	drank	Will drink	Have drunk	Would drink
You	drink	drank	Will drink	Have drunk	Would drink
He	drinks	drank	Will drink	Has drunk	Would drink
She	drinks	drank	Will drink	Has drunk	Would drink
We	drink	drank	Will drink	Have drunk	Would drink
You	drink	drank	Will drink	Have drunk	Would drink
They	drink	drank	Will drink	Have drunk	Would drink
It	drinks	drank	Will drink	Has drunk	Would drink

El método de aprendizaje South Beach para inglés conversacional

Verbos esenciales en el idioma inglés

Buscar: To Seek, To Search

	Presente	Pasado	Futuro	Participio	Condicional
I	seek	seeked	Will seek	Have seeked	Would seek
You	seek	seeked	Will seek	Have seeked	Would seek
He	seeks	seekd	Will seek	Has seeked	Would seek
She	seeks	seekd	Will seek	Has seeked	Would seek
We	seek	seekd	Will seek	Have seeked	Would seek
You	seek	seekd	Will seek	Have seeked	Would seek
They	seek	seeked	Will seek	Have seeked	Would seek
It	seeks	seeked	Will seek	Has seeked	Would seek

Caminar: To Walk

	Presente	Pasado	Futuro	Participio	Condicional
I	walk	Walked	Will walk	Have walked	Would walk
You	walk	Walked	Will walk	Have walked	Would walk
He	walks	Walked	Will walk	Has walked	Would walk
She	walks	Walked	Will walk	Has walked	Would walk
We	walk	Walked	Will walk	Have walked	Would walk
You	walk	Walked	Will walk	Have walked	Would walk
They	walk	Walked	Will walk	Have walked	Would walk
It	walks	walked	Will walk	Has walked	Would walk

Comer: To Eat

	Presente	Pasado	Futuro	Participio	Condicional
I	eat	ate	Will eat	Have ate	Would eat
You	eat	Ate	Will eat	Have ate	Would eat
He	eats	ate	Will eat	Has ate	Would eat
She	eats	ate	Will eat	Has ate	Would eat
We	eat	ate	Will eat	Have ate	Would eat
You	eat	ate	Will eat	Have ate	Would eat
They	eat	ate	Will eat	Have ate	Would eat
It	eats	ate	Will eat	Has ate	Would eat

El método de aprendizaje South Beach para inglés conversacional

Verbos esenciales en el idioma inglés

Copiar: To Copy

	Presente	Pasado	Futuro	Participio	Condicional
I	copy	copied	Will copy	Have copied	Would copy
You	copy	copied	Will copy	Have copied	Would copy
He	copies	copied	Will copy	Has copied	Would copy
She	copies	copied	Will copy	Has copied	Would copy
We	copy	copied	Will copy	Have copied	Would copy
You	copy	copied	Will copy	Have copied	Would copy
They	copy	copied	Will copy	Have copied	Would copy
It	copies	copied	Will copy	Has copied	Would copy

Correr: To Run

	Presente	Pasado	Futuro	Participio	Condicional
I	run	Ran	Will run	Have run	Would run
You	run	Ran	Will run	Have run	Would run
He	runs	Ran	Will run	Has run	Would run
She	runs	Ran	Will run	Has run	Would run
We	run	Ran	Will run	Have run	Would run
You	run	Ran	Will run	Have run	Would run
They	run	Ran	Will run	Have run	Would run
It	runs	ran	Will run	Has run	Would run

Creer: To Believe

	Presente	Pasado	Futuro	Participio	Condicional
I	believe	Believed	Will believe	Have believed	Would believe
You	believe	Believed	Will believe	Have believed	Would believe
He	believes	Believed	Will believe	Has believed	Would believe
She	believes	Believed	Will believe	Has believed	Would believe
We	believe	Believed	Will believe	Have believed	Would believe
You	believe	Believed	Will believe	Have believed	Would believe
They	believe	Believed	Will believe	Have believed	Would believe
It	believes	believed	Will believe	Has believed	Would believe

El método de aprendizaje South Beach para inglés conversacional

Verbos esenciales en el idioma inglés

Crecer: To Grow

	Presente	Pasado	Futuro	Participio	Condicional
I	grow	grew	Will grow	Have grown	Would grow
You	grow	grew	Will grow	Have grown	Would grow
He	grows	grew	Will grow	Has grown	Would grow
She	grows	grew	Will grow	Has grown	Would grow
We	grow	grew	Will grow	Have grown	Would grow
You	grow	grew	Will grow	Have grown	Would grow
They	grow	grew	Will grow	Have grown	Would grow
It	grows	grew	Will grow	Has grown	Would grow

Cocinar: To Cook

	Presente	Pasado	Futuro	Participio	Condicional
I	cook	cooked	Will cook	Have cooked	Would cook
You	cook	cooked	Will cook	Have cooked	Would cook
He	cooks	cooked	Will cook	Has cooked	Would cook
She	cooks	cooked	Will cook	Has cooked	Would cook
We	cook	cooked	Will cook	Have cooked	Would cook
You	cook	cooked	Will cook	Have cooked	Would cook
They	cook	cooked	Will cook	Have cooked	Would cook
It	cooks	cooked	Will cook	Has cooked	Would cook

Conducir: To Drive

	Presente	Pasado	Futuro	Participio	Condicional
I	drive	drove	Will drive	Have driven	Would drive
You	drive	drove	Will drive	Have driven	Would drive
He	drives	drove	Will drive	Has driven	Would drive
She	drives	drove	Will drive	Has driven	Would drive
We	drive	drove	Will drive	Have driven	Would drive
You	drive	drove	Will drive	Have driven	Would drive
They	drive	drove	Will drive	Have driven	Would drive
It	drives	drove	Will drive	Has driven	Would drive

El método de aprendizaje South Beach para inglés conversacional

Verbos esenciales en el idioma inglés

Conseguir: To Get

	Presente	Pasado	Futuro	Participio	Condicional
I	get	got	Will get	Have gotten	Would get
You	get	got	Will get	Have gotten	Would get
He	gets	got	Will get	Has gotten	Would get
She	gets	got	Will get	Has gotten	Would get
We	get	got	Will get	Have gotten	Would get
You	get	got	Will get	Have gotten	Would get
They	get	got	Will get	Have gotten	Would get
It	gets	got	Will get	Has gotten	Would get

Construir: To Build

	Presente	Pasado	Futuro	Participio	Condicional
I	Build	built	Will build	Have built	Would build
You	Build	built	Will build	Have built	Would build
He	Builds	built	Will build	Has built	Would build
She	Builds	built	Will build	Has built	Would build
We	Build	built	Will build	Have built	Would build
You	Build	built	Will build	Have built	Would build
They	Build	built	Will build	Have built	Would build
It	builds	built	Will build	Has built	Would build

Convertir: To Become

	Presente	Pasado	Futuro	Participio	Condicional
I	become	became	Will become	Have become	Would become
You	become	became	Will become	Have become	Would become
He	becomes	became	Will become	Has become	Would become
She	becomes	became	Will become	Has become	Would become
We	become	became	Will become	Have become	Would become
You	become	became	Will become	Have become	Would become
They	become	became	Will become	Have become	Would become
It	becomes	became	Will become	Has become	Would become

El método de aprendizaje South Beach para inglés conversacional

Verbos esenciales en el idioma inglés

Cerrar: To Close, To Zip

	Presente	**Pasado**	**Futuro**	**Participio**	**Condicional**
I	close	closed	Will close	Have closed	Would close
You	close	closed	Will close	Have closed	Would close
He	closes	closed	Will close	Has closed	Would close
She	closes	closed	Will close	Has closed	Would close
We	close	closed	Will close	Have closed	Would close
You	close	closed	Will close	Have closed	Would close
They	close	closed	Will close	Have closed	Would close
It	closes	closed	Will close	Has closed	Would close

Completar: To Complete

	Presente	**Pasado**	**Futuro**	**Participio**	**Condicional**
I	complete	completed	Will complete	Have completed	Would complete
You	complete	completed	Will complete	Have completed	Would complete
He	completes	completed	Will complete	Has completed	Would complete
She	completes	completed	Will complete	Has completed	Would complete
We	complete	completed	Will complete	Have completed	Would complete
You	complete	completed	Will complete	Have completed	Would complete
They	complete	completed	Will complete	Have completed	Would complete
It	completes	completed	Will complete	Has completed	Would complete

Comprar: To Buy, To Purchase

	Presente	**Pasado**	**Futuro**	**Participio**	**Condicional**
I	buy	bought	Will buy	Have bought	Would buy
You	buy	bought	Will buy	Have bought	Would buy
He	buys	bought	Will buy	Has bought	Would buy
She	buys	bought	Will buy	Has bought	Would buy
We	buy	bought	Will buy	Have bought	Would buy
You	buy	bought	Will buy	Have bought	Would buy
They	buy	bought	Will buy	Have bought	Would buy
It	buys	bought	Will buy	Has bought	Would buy

El método de aprendizaje South Beach para inglés conversacional

Verbos esenciales en el idioma inglés

Cumplir: To Keep

	Presente	Pasado	Futuro	Participio	Condicional
I	keep	kept	Will keep	Have kept	Would keep
You	keep	kept	Will keep	Have kept	Would keep
He	keeps	kept	Will keep	Has kept	Would keep
She	keeps	kept	Will keep	Has kept	Would keep
We	keep	kept	Will keep	Have kept	Would keep
You	keep	kept	Will keep	Have kept	Would keep
They	keep	kept	Will keep	Have kept	Would keep
It	keeps	kept	Will keep	Has kept	Would keep

Dar: To Give

	Presente	Pasado	Futuro	Participio	Condicional
I	give	gave	Will give	Have given	Would give
You	give	gave	Will give	Have given	Would give
He	gives	gave	Will give	Has given	Would give
She	gives	gave	Will give	Has given	Would give
We	give	gave	Will give	Have given	Would give
You	give	gave	Will give	Have given	Would give
They	give	gave	Will give	Have given	Would give
It	gives	gave	Will give	Has given	Would give

Darse Cuenta: To Realize

	Presente	Pasado	Futuro	Participio	Condicional
I	realize	realized	Will realize	Have realized	Would realize
You	realize	realized	Will realize	Have realized	Would realize
He	realizes	realized	Will realize	Has realized	Would realize
She	realizes	realized	Will realize	Has realized	Would realize
We	realize	realized	Will realize	Have realized	Would realize
You	realize	realized	Will realize	Have realized	Would realize
They	realize	realized	Will realize	Have realized	Would realize
It	realizes	realized	Will realize	Has realized	Would realize

El método de aprendizaje South Beach para inglés conversacional

Verbos esenciales en el idioma inglés

Deber: Must, To Owe (Deuda), Shall

Present		Pasado	Futuro	Participio	Condicional
I	Owe	Owed	Will Owe	Have Owed	Would Owe
You	Owe	Owed	Will Owe	Have Owed	Would Owe
He	Owes	Owed	Will Owe	Has Owed	Would Owe
She	Owes	Owed	Will Owe	Has Owed	Would Owe
We	Owe	Owed	Will Owe	Have Owed	Would Owe
You	Owe	Owed	Will Owe	Have Owed	Would Owe
They	Owe	Owed	Will Owe	Have Owed	Would Owe
It	Owes	Owed	Will Owe	Has Owed	Would Owe

Deber: Must, To Owe (Deuda), Shall

Presente		Pasado	Futuro	Participio	Condicional
I	Must				
You	Must				
He	Must				
She	Must				
We	Must				
You	Must				
They	Must				
It	Must				

Deber: Must, To Owe (Deuda), Shall

	Presente	Pasado	Futuro	Participio	Condicional
	Shall				Should Should
I	Shall				Should Should
You	Shall				Should Should
He	Shall				Should Should
She	Shall				
We	Shall				
You	Shall				
They	Shall				
It					

El método de aprendizaje South Beach para inglés conversacional

Verbos esenciales en el idioma inglés

Debería: Should

	Presente	Pasado	Futuro	Participio	Condicional
I					Should
You					Should
He					Should
She					Should
We					Should
You					Should
They					Should
It					Should

Decir: To Say, To Tell

	Presente	Pasado	Futuro	Participio	Condicional
I	Say	Said	Will Say	Have Said	Would Say
You	Say	Said	Will Say	Have Said	Would Say
He	Says	Said	Will Say	Has Said	Would Say
She	Says	Said	Will Say	Has Said	Would Say
We	Say	Said	Will Say	Have Said	Would Say
You	Say	Said	Will Say	Have Said	Would Say
They	Say	Said	Will Say	Have Said	Would Say
It	Says	Said	Will Say	Has Said	Would Say

Decir: To Say, To Tell

	Presente	Pasado	Futuro	Participio	Condicional
I	Tell	Told	Will Tell	Have Told	Would Tell
You	Tell	Told	Will Tell	Have Told	Would Tell
He	Tells	Told	Will Tell	Has Told	Would Tell
She	Tells	Told	Will Tell	Has Told	Would Tell
We	Tell	Told	Will Tell	Have Told	Would Tell
You	Tell	Told	Will Tell	Have Told	Would Tell
They	Tell	Told	Will Tell	Have Told	Would Tell
It	Tells	Told	Will Tell	Has Told	Would Tell

El método de aprendizaje South Beach para inglés conversacional

Verbos esenciales en el idioma inglés

Dejar: To Let, To Leave, To Abandon

	Presente	Pasado	Futuro	Participio	Condicional
I	Let	Let	Will Let	Have Let	Would Let
You	Let	Let	Will Let	Have Let	Would Let
He	Lets	Let	Will Let	Has Let	Would Let
She	Lets	Let	Will Let	Has Let	Would Let
We	Let	Let	Will Let	Have Let	Would Let
You	Let	Let	Will Let	Have Let	Would Let
They	Let	Let	Will Let	Have Let	Would Let
It	Lets	Let	Will Let	Has Let	Would Let

Dejar: To Let, To Leave, To Abandon

	Presente	Pasado	Futuro	Participio	Condicional
I	Leave	Left	Will Leave	Have Left	Would Leave
You	Leave	Left	Will Leave	Have Left	Would Leave
He	Leaves	Left	Will Leave	Has Left	Would Leave
She	Leaves	Left	Will Leave	Has Left	Would Leave
We	Leave	Left	Will Leave	Have Left	Would Leave
You	Leave	Left	Will Leave	Have Left	Would Leave
They	Leave	Left	Will Leave	Have Left	Would Leave
It	Leaves	Left	Will Leave	Has Left	Would Leave

Dejar: To Let, To Leave, To Abandon

	Presente	Pasado	Futuro	Participio	Condicional
I	Abandon	Abandoned	Will Abandon	Have Abandoned	Would Abandon
You	Abandon	Abandoned	Will Abandon	Have Abandoned	Would Abandon
He	Abandons	Abandoned	Will Abandon	Has Abandoned	Would Abandon
She	Abandons	Abandoned	Will Abandon	Has Abandoned	Would Abandon
We	Abandon	Abandoned	Will Abandon	Have Abandoned	Would Abandon
You	Abandon	Abandoned	Will Abandon	Have Abandoned	Would Abandon
They	Abandon	Abandoned	Will Abandon	Have Abandoned	Would Abandon
It	Abandons	Abandoned	Will Abandon	Has Abandoned	Would Abandon

El método de aprendizaje South Beach para inglés conversacional

Verbos esenciales en el idioma inglés

Desear: To Wish

	Presente	**Pasado**	**Futuro**	**Participio**	**Condicional**
I	wish	wished	Will wish	Have wished	Would wish
You	wish	wished	Will wish	Have wished	Would wish
He	wishes	wished	Will wish	Has wished	Would wish
She	wishes	wished	Will wish	Has wished	Would wish
We	wish	wished	Will wish	Have wished	Would wish
You	wish	wished	Will wish	Have wished	Would wish
They	wish	wished	Will wish	Have wished	Would wish
It	wishes	wished	Will wish	Has wished	Would wish

Discutir: To Argue, To Discuss

	Presente	**Pasado**	**Futuro**	**Participio**	**Condicional**
I	argue	argued	Will argue	Have argued	Would argue
You	argue	argued	Will argue	Have argued	Would argue
He	argues	argued	Will argue	Has argued	Would argue
She	argues	argued	Will argue	Has argued	Would argue
We	argue	argued	Will argue	Have argued	Would argue
You	argue	argued	Will argue	Have argued	Would argue
They	argue	argued	Will argue	Have argued	Would argue
It	argues	argued	Will argue	Has argued	Would argue

Discutir: To Argue, To Discuss

	Presente	**Pasado**	**Futuro**	**Participio**	**Condicional**
I	discuss	discussed	Will discuss	Have discussed	Would discuss
You	discuss	discussed	Will discuss	Have discussed	Would discuss
He	discusss	discussed	Will discuss	Has discussed	Would discuss
She	discusss	discussed	Will discuss	Has discussed	Would discuss
We	discuss	discussed	Will discuss	Have discussed	Would discuss
You	discuss	discussed	Will discuss	Have discussed	Would discuss
They	discuss	discussed	Will discuss	Have discussed	Would discuss
It	discusss	discussed	Will discuss	Has discussed	Would discuss

El método de aprendizaje South Beach para inglés conversacional

Verbos esenciales en el idioma inglés

Dormir: To Sleep

	Presente	Pasado	Futuro	Participio	Condicional
I	sleep	slept	Will sleep	Have slept	Would sleep
You	sleep	slept	Will sleep	Have slept	Would sleep
He	sleepes	slept	Will sleep	Has slept	Would sleep
She	sleepes	slept	Will sleep	Has slept	Would sleep
We	sleep	slept	Will sleep	Have slept	Would sleep
You	sleep	slept	Will sleep	Have slept	Would sleep
They	sleep	slept	Will sleep	Have slept	Would sleep
It	sleepes	slept	Will sleep	Has slept	Would sleep

Dudar: To Doubt

	Presente	Pasado	Futuro	Participio	Condicional
I	doubt	doubted	Will doubt	Have doubted	Would doubt
You	doubt	doubted	Will doubt	Have doubted	Would doubt
He	doubts	doubted	Will doubt	Has doubted	Would doubt
She	doubts	doubted	Will doubt	Has doubted	Would doubt
We	doubt	doubted	Will doubt	Have doubted	Would doubt
You	doubt	doubted	Will doubt	Have doubted	Would doubt
They	doubt	doubted	Will doubt	Have doubted	Would doubt
It	doubts	doubted	Will doubt	Has doubted	Would doubt

Devengar: To Earn

	Presente	Pasado	Futuro	Participio	Condicional
I	earn	earned	Will earn	Have earned	Would earn
You	earn	earned	Will earn	Have earned	Would earn
He	earns	earned	Will earn	Has earned	Would earn
She	earns	earned	Will earn	Has earned	Would earn
We	earn	earned	Will earn	Have earned	Would earn
You	earn	earned	Will earn	Have earned	Would earn
They	earn	earned	Will earn	Have earned	Would earn
It	earns	earned	Will earn	Has earned	Would earn

El método de aprendizaje South Beach para inglés conversacional

Verbos esenciales en el idioma inglés

Demostrar: To Demonstrate, To Show

	Presente	**Pasado**	**Futuro**	**Participio**	**Condicional**
I	show	showed	Will show	Have showed	Would show
You	show	showed	Will show	Have showed	Would show
He	shows	showed	Will show	Has showed	Would show
She	shows	showed	Will show	Has showed	Would show
We	show	showed	Will show	Have showed	Would show
You	show	showed	Will show	Have showed	Would show
They	show	showed	Will show	Have showed	Would show
It	shows	showed	Will show	Has showed	Would show

Ser dueño de: To Own

	Presente	**Pasado**	**Futuro**	**Participio**	**Condicional**
I	own	owned	Will own	Have owned	Would own
You	own	owned	Will own	Have owned	Would own
He	owns	owned	Will own	Has owned	Would own
She	owns	owned	Will own	Has owned	Would own
We	own	owned	Will own	Have owned	Would own
You	own	owned	Will own	Have owned	Would own
They	own	owned	Will own	Have owned	Would own
It	owns	owned	Will own	Has owned	Would own

Empezar: To Start, To Begin

	Presente	**Pasado**	**Futuro**	**Participio**	**Condicional**
I	start	started	Will start	Have started	Would start
You	start	started	Will start	Have started	Would start
He	starts	started	Will start	Has started	Would start
She	starts	started	Will start	Has started	Would start
We	start	started	Will start	Have started	Would start
You	start	started	Will start	Have started	Would start
They	start	started	Will start	Have started	Would start
It	starts	started	Will start	Has started	Would start

El método de aprendizaje South Beach para inglés conversacional

Verbos esenciales en el idioma inglés

Empujar: To Push

	Presente	Pasado	Futuro	Participio	Condicional
I	push	pushed	Will push	Have pushed	Would push
You	push	pushed	Will push	Have pushed	Would push
He	pushs	pushed	Will push	Has pushed	Would push
She	pushs	pushed	Will push	Has pushed	Would push
We	push	pushed	Will push	Have pushed	Would push
You	push	pushed	Will push	Have pushed	Would push
They	push	pushed	Will push	Have pushed	Would push
It	pushs	pushed	Will push	Has pushed	Would push

Encontrar: To Find

	Presente	Pasado	Futuro	Participio	Condicional
I	find	found	Will find	Have found	Would find
You	find	found	Will find	Have found	Would find
He	finds	found	Will find	Has found	Would find
She	finds	found	Will find	Has found	Would find
We	find	found	Will find	Have found	Would find
You	find	found	Will find	Have found	Would find
They	find	found	Will find	Have found	Would find
It	finds	found	Will find	Has found	Would find

Enseñar: To Teach

	Presente	Pasado	Futuro	Participio	Condicional
I	teach	taught	Will teach	Have taught	Would teach
You	teach	taught	Will teach	Have taught	Would teach
He	teaches	taught	Will teach	Has taught	Would teach
She	teaches	taught	Will teach	Has taught	Would teach
We	teach	taught	Will teach	Have taught	Would teach
You	teach	taught	Will teach	Have taught	Would teach
They	teach	taught	Will teach	Have taught	Would teach
It	teaches	taught	Will teach	Has taught	Would teach

El método de aprendizaje South Beach para inglés conversacional

Verbos esenciales en el idioma inglés

Enviar: To Send

	Presente	**Pasado**	**Futuro**	**Participio**	**Condicional**
I	send	sent	Will send	Have sent	Would send
You	send	sent	Will send	Have sent	Would send
He	sends	sent	Will send	Has sent	Would send
She	sends	sent	Will send	Has sent	Would send
We	send	sent	Will send	Have sent	Would send
You	send	sent	Will send	Have sent	Would send
They	send	sent	Will send	Have sent	Would send
It	sends	sent	Will send	Has sended	Would show

Entender: To Understand

	Presente	**Pasado**	**Futuro**	**Participio**	**Condicional**
I	understand	understood	Will understand	Have understood	Would understand
You	understand	understood	Will understand	Have understood	Would understand
He	understands	understood	Will understand	Has understood	Would understand
She	understands	understood	Will understand	Has understood	Would understand
We	understand	understood	Will understand	Have understood	Would understand
You	understand	understood	Will understand	Have understood	Would understand
They	understand	understood	Will understand	Have understood	Would understand
It	understands	understood	Will understand	Has understood	Would understand

Entrar: To Enter

	Presente	**Pasado**	**Futuro**	**Participio**	**Condicional**
I	enter	entered	Will enter	Have entered	Would enter
You	enter	entered	Will enter	Have entered	Would enter
He	enters	entered	Will enter	Has entered	Would enter
She	enters	entered	Will enter	Has entered	Would enter
We	enter	entered	Will enter	Have entered	Would enter
You	enter	entered	Will enter	Have entered	Would enter
They	enter	entered	Will enter	Have entered	Would enter
It	enters	entered	Will enter	Has entered	Would enter

El método de aprendizaje South Beach para inglés conversacional

Verbos esenciales en el idioma inglés

Escoger: To Pick

	Presente	Pasado	Futuro	Participio	Condicional
I	pick	picked	Will pick	Have picked	Would pick
You	pick	picked	Will pick	Have picked	Would pick
He	picks	picked	Will pick	Has picked	Would pick
She	picks	picked	Will pick	Has picked	Would pick
We	pick	picked	Will pick	Have picked	Would pick
You	pick	picked	Will pick	Have picked	Would pick
They	pick	picked	Will pick	Have picked	Would pick
It	picks	picked	Will pick	Has picked	Would pick

Escribir: To Write

	Presente	Pasado	Futuro	Participio	Condicional
I	write	wrote	Will write	Have written	Would write
You	write	wrote	Will write	Have written	Would write
He	writes	wrote	Will write	Has written	Would write
She	writes	wrote	Will write	Has written	Would write
We	write	wrote	Will write	Have written	Would write
You	write	wrote	Will write	Have written	Would write
They	write	wrote	Will write	Have written	Would write
It	writes	wrote	Will write	Has written	Would write

Esperar: To Wait

	Presente	Pasado	Futuro	Participio	Condicional
I	wait	waited	Will wait	Have waited	Would wait
You	wait	waited	Will wait	Have waited	Would wait
He	waits	waited	Will wait	Has waited	Would wait
She	waits	waited	Will wait	Has waited	Would wait
We	wait	waited	Will wait	Have waited	Would wait
You	wait	waited	Will wait	Have waited	Would wait
They	wait	waited	Will wait	Have waited	Would wait
It	waits	waited	Will wait	Has waited	Would wait

El método de aprendizaje South Beach para inglés conversacional

Verbos esenciales en el idioma inglés

Estar: To Be

	Presente	Pasado	Futuro	Participio	Condicional
I	Am	Was	Will Be	Have Been	Would Be
You	Are	Were	Will Be	Have Been	Would Be
He	Is	Was	Will Be	Has Been	Would Be
She	Is	Was	Will Be	Has Been	Would Be
We	Are	Were	Will Be	Have Been	Would Be
You	Are	Were	Will Be	Have Been	Would Be
They	Are	Were	Will Be	Have Been	Would Be
It	Is	Was	Will Be	Has Been	Would Be

Estar agradecido: To Be Thankful

	Presente	Pasado	Futuro	Participio	Condicional
I	Am Thankful	Was Thankful	Will Be Thankful	Have Been Thankful	Would Be Thankful
You	Are Thankful	Were Thankful	Will Be Thankful	Have Been Thankful	Would Be Thankful
He	Is Thankful	Was Thankful	Will Be Thankful	Has Been Thankful	Would Be Thankful
She	Is Thankful	Was Thankful	Will Be Thankful	Has Been Thankful	Would Be Thankful
We	Are Thankful	Were Thankful	Will Be Thankful	Have Been Thankful	Would Be Thankful
You	Are Thankful	Were Thankful	Will Be Thankful	Have Been Thankful	Would Be Thankful
They	Are Thankful	Were Thankful	Will Be Thankful	Have Been Thankful	Would Be Thankful
It	Is Thankful	Was Thankful	Will Be Thankful	Has Been Thankful	Would Be Thankful

Estar molesto: To Be Angry

	Presente	Pasado	Futuro	Participio	Condicional
I	Am Angry	Was Angry	Will Be Angry	Have Been Angry	Would Be Angry
You	Are Angry	Were Angry	Will Be Angry	Have Been Angry	Would Be Angry
He	Is Angry	Was Angry	Will Be Angry	Has Been Angry	Would Be Angry
She	Is Angry	Was Angry	Will Be Angry	Has Been Angry	Would Be Angry
We	Are Angry	Were Angry	Will Be Angry	Have Been Angry	Would Be Angry
You	Are Angry	Were Angry	Will Be Angry	Have Been Angry	Would Be Angry
They	Are Angry	Were Angry	Will Be Angry	Have Been Angry	Would Be Angry
It	Is Angry	Was Angry	Will Be Angry	Has Been Angry	Would Be Angry

El método de aprendizaje South Beach para inglés conversacional

Verbos esenciales en el idioma inglés

Estar Equivocado: To be wrong

	Presente	Pasado	Futuro	Participio	Condicional
I	Am Wrong	Was Wrong	Will Be Wrong	Have Been Wrong	Would Be Wrong
You	Are Wrong	Were Wrong	Will Be Wrong	Have Been Wrong	Would Be Wrong
He	Is Wrong	Was Wrong	Will Be Wrong	Has Been Wrong	Would Be Wrong
She	Is Wrong	Was Wrong	Will Be Wrong	Has Been Wrong	Would Be Wrong
We	Are Wrong	Were Wrong	Will Be Wrong	Have Been Wrong	Would Be Wrong
You	Are Wrong	Were Wrong	Will Be Wrong	Have Been Wrong	Would Be Wrong
They	Are Wrong	Were Wrong	Will Be Wrong	Have Been Wrong	Would Be Wrong
It	Is Wrong	Was Wrong	Will Be Wrong	Has Been Wrong	Would Be Wrong

Estudiar: To Study

	Presente	Pasado	Futuro	Participio	Condicional
I	Study	Studied	Will Study	Have Studied	Would Study
You	Study	Studied	Will Study	Have Studied	Would Study
He	Studies	Studied	Will Study	Has Studied	Would Study
She	Studies	Studied	Will Study	Has Studied	Would Study
We	Study	Studied	Will Study	Have Studied	Would Study
You	Study	Studied	Will Study	Have Studied	Would Study
They	Study	Studied	Will Study	Have Studied	Would Study
It	Studies	Studied	Will Study	Has Studied	Would Study

Escuchar: To Listen

	Presente	Pasado	Futuro	Participio	Condicional
I	Listen	Listened	Will Listen	Have Listened	Would Listen
You	Listen	Listened	Will Listen	Have Listened	Would Listen
He	Listens	Listened	Will Listen	Has Listened	Would Listen
She	Listens	Listened	Will Listen	Has Listened	Would Listen
We	Listen	Listened	Will Listen	Have Listened	Would Listen
You	Listen	Listened	Will Listen	Have Listened	Would Listen
They	Listen	Listened	Will Listen	Have Listened	Would Listen
It	Listens	Listened	Will Listen	Has Listened	Would Listen

El método de aprendizaje South Beach para inglés conversacional

Verbos esenciales en el idioma inglés

Favorecer: To Favor

	Presente	**Pasado**	**Futuro**	**Participio**	**Condicional**
I	favour	favoured	Will favour	Have favoured	Would favour
You	favour	favoured	Will favour	Have favoured	Would favour
He	favours	favoured	Will favour	Has favoured	Would favour
She	favours	favoured	Will favour	Has favoured	Would favour
We	favour	favoured	Will favour	Have favoured	Would favour
You	favour	favoured	Will favour	Have favoured	Would favour
They	favour	favoured	Will favour	Have favoured	Would favour
It	favours	favoured	Will favour	Has favoured	Would favour

Ganar: To Earn

	Presente	**Pasado**	**Futuro**	**Participio**	**Condicional**
I	earn	earned	Will earn	Have earned	Would earn
You	earn	earned	Will earn	Have earned	Would earn
He	earns	earned	Will earn	Has earned	Would earn
She	earns	earned	Will earn	Has earned	Would earn
We	earn	earned	Will earn	Have earned	Would earn
You	earn	earned	Will earn	Have earned	Would earn
They	earn	earned	Will earn	Have earned	Would earn
It	earns	earned	Will earn	Has earned	Would earn

Ganar: To Win

	Presente	**Pasado**	**Futuro**	**Participio**	**Condicional**
I	win	won	Will win	Have won	Would win
You	win	won	Will win	Have won	Would win
He	wins	won	Will win	Has won	Would win
She	wins	won	Will win	Has won	Would win
We	win	won	Will win	Have won	Would win
You	win	won	Will win	Have won	Would win
They	win	won	Will win	Have won	Would win
It	wins	won	Will win	Has won	Would win

El método de aprendizaje South Beach para inglés conversacional

Verbos esenciales en el idioma inglés

Gustar: To Like

	Presente	Pasado	Futuro	Participio	Condicional
I	like	liked	Will like	Have liked	Would like
You	like	liked	Will like	Have liked	Would like
He	likes	liked	Will like	Has liked	Would like
She	likes	liked	Will like	Has liked	Would like
We	like	liked	Will like	Have liked	Would like
You	like	liked	Will like	Have liked	Would like
They	like	liked	Will like	Have liked	Would like
It	likes	liked	Will like	Has liked	Would like

Haber: To Have

	Presente	Pasado	Futuro	Participio	Condicional
I	have	had	Will have	Have had	Would have
You	have	had	Will have	Have had	Would have
He	has	had	Will have	Has had	Would have
She	has	had	Will have	Has had	Would have
We	have	had	Will have	Have had	Would have
You	have	had	Will have	Have had	Would have
They	have	had	Will have	Have had	Would have
It	has	had	Will have	Has had	Would have

Hablar: To Talk

	Presente	Pasado	Futuro	Participio	Condicional
I	talk	talked	Will talk	Have talked	Would talk
You	talk	talked	Will talk	Have talked	Would talk
He	talks	talked	Will talk	Has talked	Would talk
She	talks	talked	Will talk	Has talked	Would talk
We	talk	talked	Will talk	Have talked	Would talk
You	talk	talked	Will talk	Have talked	Would talk
They	talk	talked	Will talk	Have talked	Would talk
It	talks	talked	Will talk	Has talked	Would talk

El método de aprendizaje South Beach para inglés conversacional

Verbos esenciales en el idioma inglés

Hablar: To Speak

	Presente	Pasado	Futuro	Participio	Condicional
I	speak	spoke	Will speak	Have spoken	Would speak
You	speak	spoke	Will speak	Have spoken	Would speak
He	speaks	spoke	Will speak	Has spoken	Would speak
She	speaks	spoke	Will speak	Has spoken	Would speak
We	speak	spoke	Will speak	Have spoken	Would speak
You	speak	spoke	Will speak	Have spoken	Would speak
They	speak	spoke	Will speak	Have spoken	Would speak
It	speaks	spoke	Will speak	Has spoken	Would speak

Hacer: To Do

	Presente	Pasado	Futuro	Participio	Condicional
I	do	did	Will do	do done	Would do
You	do	did	Will do	do done	Would do
He	does	did	Will do	Has done	Would do
She	does	did	Will do	Has done	Would do
We	do	did	Will do	do done	Would do
You	do	did	Will do	do done	Would do
They	do	did	Will do	do done	Would do
It	does	did	Will do	Has done	Would do

Halar: To Pull

	Presente	Pasado	Futuro	Participio	Condicional
I	pull	pulled	Will pull	Have pulled	Would pull
You	pull	pulled	Will pull	Have pulled	Would pull
He	pulls	pulled	Will pull	Has pulled	Would pull
She	pulls	pulled	Will pull	Has pulled	Would pull
We	pull	pulled	Will pull	Have pulled	Would pull
You	pull	pulled	Will pull	Have pulled	Would pull
They	pull	pulled	Will pull	Have pulled	Would pull
It	pulls	pulled	Will pull	Has pulled	Would pull

El método de aprendizaje South Beach para inglés conversacional

Verbos esenciales en el idioma inglés

Ir de compras: To Shop

	Presente	Pasado	Futuro	Participio	Condicional
I	shop	shopped	Will shop	Have shopped	Would shop
You	shop	shopped	Will shop	Have shopped	Would shop
He	shops	shopped	Will shop	Has shopped	Would shop
She	shops	shopped	Will shop	Has shopped	Would shop
We	shop	shopped	Will shop	Have shopped	Would shop
You	shop	shopped	Will shop	Have shopped	Would shop
They	shop	shopped	Will shop	Have shopped	Would shop
It	shops	shopped	Will shop	Has shopped	Would shop

Ir: To Go

	Presente	Pasado	Futuro	Participio	Condicional
I	go	went	Will go	have gone	Would go
You	go	went	Will go	have gone	Would go
He	goes	went	Will go	Has gone	Would go
She	goes	went	Will go	Has gone	Would go
We	go	went	Will go	has gone	Would go
You	go	went	Will go	have gone	Would go
They	go	went	Will go	have gone	Would go
It	goes	went	Will go	Has gone	Would go

Jugar: To Play (Un juego, apostar)

	Presente	Pasado	Futuro	Participio	Condicional
I	play	played	Will play	Have played	Would play
You	play	played	Will play	Have played	Would play
He	plays	played	Will play	Has played	Would play
She	plays	played	Will play	Has played	Would play
We	play	played	Will play	Have played	Would play
You	play	played	Will play	Have played	Would play
They	play	played	Will play	Have played	Would play
It	plays	played	Will play	Has played	Would play

El método de aprendizaje South Beach para inglés conversacional

Verbos esenciales en el idioma inglés

Lavar: To Wash

	Presente	**Pasado**	**Futuro**	**Participio**	**Condicional**
I	wash	washed	Will wash	Have washed	Would wash
You	wash	washed	Will wash	Have washed	Would wash
He	washs	washed	Will wash	Has washed	Would wash
She	washs	washed	Will wash	Has washed	Would wash
We	wash	washed	Will wash	Have washed	Would wash
You	wash	washed	Will wash	Have washed	Would wash
They	wash	washed	Will wash	Have washed	Would wash
It	washs	washed	Will wash	Has washed	Would wash

Leer: To Read

	Presente	**Pasado**	**Futuro**	**Participio**	**Condicional**
I	read	read	Will read	Have read	Would read
You	read	read	Will read	Have read	Would read
He	reads	read	Will read	Has read	Would read
She	reads	read	Will read	Has read	Would read
We	read	read	Will read	Have read	Would read
You	read	read	Will read	Have read	Would read
They	read	read	Will read	Have read	Would read
It	reads	read	Will read	Has read	Would read

Limpiar: To Clean

	Presente	**Pasado**	**Futuro**	**Participio**	**Condicional**
I	clean	cleaned	Will clean	Have cleaned	Would clean
You	clean	cleaned	Will clean	Have cleaned	Would clean
He	cleans	cleaned	Will clean	Has cleaned	Would clean
She	cleans	cleaned	Will clean	Has cleaned	Would clean
We	clean	cleaned	Will clean	Have cleaned	Would clean
You	clean	cleaned	Will clean	Have cleaned	Would clean
They	clean	cleaned	Will clean	Have cleaned	Would clean
It	cleans	cleaned	Will clean	Has cleaned	Would clean

El método de aprendizaje South Beach para inglés conversacional

Verbos esenciales en el idioma inglés

Llamar: To Call

	Presente	Pasado	Futuro	Participio	Condicional
I	call	called	Will call	Have called	Would call
You	call	called	Will call	Have called	Would call
He	calls	called	Will call	Has called	Would call
She	calls	called	Will call	Has called	Would call
We	call	called	Will call	Have called	Would call
You	call	called	Will call	Have called	Would call
They	call	called	Will call	Have called	Would call
It	calls	called	Will call	Has called	Would call

Llegar: To Arrive

	Presente	Pasado	Futuro	Participio	Condicional
I	arrive	arrived	Will arrive	Have arrived	Would arrive
You	arrive	arrived	Will arrive	Have arrived	Would arrive
He	arrives	arrived	Will arrive	Has arrived	Would arrive
She	arrives	arrived	Will arrive	Has arrived	Would arrive
We	arrive	arrived	Will arrive	Have arrived	Would arrive
You	arrive	arrived	Will arrive	Have arrived	Would arrive
They	arrive	arrived	Will arrive	Have arrived	Would arrive
It	arrives	arrived	Will arrive	Has arrived	Would arrive

Llevar: To Take

	Presente	Pasado	Futuro	Participio	Condicional
I	take	took	Will take	Have taken	Would take
You	take	took	Will take	Have taken	Would take
He	takes	took	Will take	Has taken	Would take
She	takes	took	Will take	Has taken	Would take
We	take	took	Will take	Have taken	Would take
You	take	took	Will take	Have taken	Would take
They	take	took	Will take	Have taken	Would take
It	takes	took	Will take	Has taken	Would take

El método de aprendizaje South Beach para inglés conversacional

Verbos esenciales en el idioma inglés

Lograr, Obtener, Recibir: To Get

	Presente	Pasado	Futuro	Participio	Condicional
I	get	got	Will get	Have gotten	Would get
You	get	got	Will get	Have gotten	Would get
He	gets	got	Will get	Has gotten	Would get
She	gets	got	Will get	Has gotten	Would get
We	get	got	Will get	Have gotten	Would get
You	get	got	Will get	Have gotten	Would get
They	get	got	Will get	Have gotten	Would get
It	gets	got	Will get	Has gotten	Would get

Mejorar: To Improve

	Presente	Pasado	Futuro	Participio	Condicional
I	improve	improved	Will improve	Have improved	Would improve
You	improve	improved	Will improve	Have improved	Would improve
He	improves	improved	Will improve	Has improved	Would improve
She	improves	improved	Will improve	Has improved	Would improve
We	improve	improved	Will improve	Have improved	Would improve
You	improve	improved	Will improve	Have improved	Would improve
They	improve	improved	Will improve	Have improved	Would improve
It	improves	improved	Will improve	Has improved	Would improve

Mantener: To Keep

	Presente	Pasado	Futuro	Participio	Condicional
I	keep	kept	Will keep	Have kept	Would keep
You	keep	kept	Will keep	Have kept	Would keep
He	keeps	kept	Will keep	Has kept	Would keep
She	keeps	kept	Will keep	Has kept	Would keep
We	keep	kept	Will keep	Have kept	Would keep
You	keep	kept	Will keep	Have kept	Would keep
They	keep	kept	Will keep	Have kept	Would keep
It	keeps	kept	Will keep	Has kept	Would keep

El método de aprendizaje South Beach para inglés conversacional

Verbos esenciales en el idioma inglés

Mostrar: To Show

	Presente	Pasado	Futuro	Participio	Condicional
I	show	showed	Will show	Have showed	Would show
You	show	showed	Will show	Have showed	Would show
He	shows	showed	Will show	Has showed	Would show
She	shows	showed	Will show	Has showed	Would show
We	show	showed	Will show	Have showed	Would show
You	show	showed	Will show	Have showed	Would show
They	show	showed	Will show	Have showed	Would show
It	shows	showed	Will show	Has showed	Would show

Mirar: To Watch, To Look

	Presente	Pasado	Futuro	Participio	Condicional
I	look	looked	Will look	Have looked	Would look
You	look	looked	Will look	Have looked	Would look
He	looks	looked	Will look	Has looked	Would look
She	looks	looked	Will look	Has looked	Would look
We	look	looked	Will look	Have looked	Would look
You	look	looked	Will look	Have looked	Would look
They	look	looked	Will look	Have looked	Would look
It	looks	looked	Will look	Has looked	Would look

Mirar: To Watch, To Look

	Presente	Pasado	Futuro	Participio	Condicional
I	watch	watched	Will watch	Have watched	Would watch
You	watch	watched	Will watch	Have watched	Would watch
He	watchs	watched	Will watch	Has watched	Would watch
She	watchs	watched	Will watch	Has watched	Would watch
We	watch	watched	Will watch	Have watched	Would watch
You	watch	watched	Will watch	Have watched	Would watch
They	watch	watched	Will watch	Have watched	Would watch
It	watchs	watched	Will watch	Has watched	Would watch

El método de aprendizaje South Beach para inglés conversacional

Verbos esenciales en el idioma inglés

Mentir: To Lie

	Presente	Pasado	Futuro	Participio	Condicional
I	lie	lied	Will lie	Have lied	Would lie
You	lie	lied	Will lie	Have lied	Would lie
He	lies	lied	Will lie	Has lied	Would lie
She	lies	lied	Will lie	Has lied	Would lie
We	lie	lied	Will lie	Have lied	Would lie
You	lie	lied	Will lie	Have lied	Would lie
They	lie	lied	Will lie	Have lied	Would lie
It	lies	lied	Will lie	Has lied	Would lie

Necesitar: To Need

	Presente	Pasado	Futuro	Participio	Condicional
I	need	needed	Will need	Have needed	Would need
You	need	needed	Will need	Have needed	Would need
He	needs	needed	Will need	Has needed	Would need
She	needs	needed	Will need	Has needed	Would need
We	need	needed	Will need	Have needed	Would need
You	need	needed	Will need	Have needed	Would need
They	need	needed	Will need	Have needed	Would need
It	needs	needed	Will need	Has needed	Would need

Obtener: To Get

	Presente	Pasado	Futuro	Participio	Condicional
I	get	got	Will get	Have gotten	Would get
You	get	got	Will get	Have gotten	Would get
He	gets	got	Will get	Has gotten	Would get
She	gets	got	Will get	Has gotten	Would get
We	get	got	Will get	Have gotten	Would get
You	get	got	Will get	Have gotten	Would get
They	get	got	Will get	Have gotten	Would get
It	gets	got	Will get	Has gotten	Would get

El método de aprendizaje South Beach para inglés conversacional

Verbos esenciales en el idioma inglés

Ofrecer: To Offer

	Presente	**Pasado**	**Futuro**	**Participio**	**Condicional**
I	offer	offered	Will offer	Have offered	Would offer
You	offer	offered	Will offer	Have offered	Would offer
He	offers	offered	Will offer	Has offered	Would offer
She	offers	offered	Will offer	Has offered	Would offer
We	offer	offered	Will offer	Have offered	Would offer
You	offer	offered	Will offer	Have offered	Would offer
They	offer	offered	Will offer	Have offered	Would offer
It	offers	offered	Will offer	Has offered	Would offer

Olvidar: To Forget

	Presente	**Pasado**	**Futuro**	**Participio**	**Condicional**
I	forget	forgot	Will forget	Have forgotten	Would forget
You	forget	forgot	Will forget	Have forgotten	Would forget
He	forgets	forgot	Will forget	Has forgotten	Would forget
She	forgets	forgot	Will forget	Has forgotten	Would forget
We	forget	forgot	Will forget	Have forgotten	Would forget
You	forget	forgot	Will forget	Have forgotten	Would forget
They	forget	forgot	Will forget	Have forgotten	Would forget
It	forgets	forgot	Will forget	Has forgotten	Would forget

Ordenar: To Order

	Presente	**Pasado**	**Futuro**	**Participio**	**Condicional**
I	order	ordered	Will order	Have ordered	Would order
You	order	ordered	Will order	Have ordered	Would order
He	orders	ordered	Will order	Has ordered	Would order
She	orders	ordered	Will order	Has ordered	Would order
We	order	ordered	Will order	Have ordered	Would order
You	order	ordered	Will order	Have ordered	Would order
They	order	ordered	Will order	Have ordered	Would order
It	orders	ordered	Will order	Has ordered	Would order

El método de aprendizaje South Beach para inglés conversacional

Verbos esenciales en el idioma inglés

P Pagar: To Pay

	Presente	Pasado	Futuro	Participio	Condicional
I	Pay	Payed	Will Pay	Have Payed	Would Pay
You	Pay	Payed	Will Pay	Have Payed	Would Pay
He	Pays	Payed	Will Pay	Has Payed	Would Pay
She	Pays	Payed	Will Pay	Has Payed	Would Pay
We	Pay	Payed	Will Pay	Have Payed	Would Pay
You	Pay	Payed	Will Pay	Have Payed	Would Pay
They	Pay	Payed	Will Pay	Have Payed	Would Pay
It	Pays	Payed	Will Pay	Has Payed	Would Pay

Parecer: To Look Like

	Presente	Pasado	Futuro	Participio	Condicional
I	Look Like	Looked Like	Will Look Like	Have Looked Like	Would Look Like
You	Look Like	Looked Like	Will Look Like	Have Looked Like	Would Look Like
He	Looks Like	Looked Like	Will Look Like	Has Looked Like	Would Look Like
She	Looks Like	Looked Like	Will Look Like	Has Looked Like	Would Look Like
We	Look Like	Looked Like	Will Look Like	Have Looked Like	Would Look Like
You	Look Like	Looked Like	Will Look Like	Have Looked Like	Would Look Like
They	Look Like	Looked Like	Will Look Like	Have Looked Like	Would Look Like
It	Looks Like	Looked Like	Will Look Like	Has Looked Like	Would Look Like

Partir: To Leave, To Depart

	Presente	Pasado	Futuro	Participio	Condicional
I	Depart	Departed	Will Depart	Have Departed	Would Depart
You	Depart	Departed	Will Depart	Have Departed	Would Depart
He	Departs	Departed	Will Depart	Has Departed	Would Depart
She	Departs	Departed	Will Depart	Has Departed	Would Depart
We	Depart	Departed	Will Depart	Have Departed	Would Depart
You	Depart	Departed	Will Depart	Have Departed	Would Depart
They	Depart	Departed	Will Depart	Have Departed	Would Depart
It	Departs	Departed	Will Depart	Has Departed	Would Depart

Verbos esenciales en el idioma inglés

Partir: To Leave, To Depart

	Presente	Pasado	Futuro	Participio	Condicional
I	leave	left	Will leave	Have left	Would leave
You	leave	left	Will leave	Have left	Would leave
He	leaves	left	Will leave	Has left	Would leave
She	leaves	left	Will leave	Has left	Would leave
We	leave	left	Will leave	Have left	Would leave
You	leave	left	Will leave	Have left	Would leave
They	leave	left	Will leave	Have left	Would leave
It	leaves	left	Will leave	Has left	Would leave

Pasar: To Happen

	Presente	Pasado	Futuro	Participio	Condicional
I	happen	happened	Will happen	Have happened	Would happen
You	happen	happened	Will happen	Have happened	Would happen
He	happens	happened	Will happen	Has happened	Would happen
She	happens	happened	Will happen	Has happened	Would happen
We	happen	happened	Will happen	Have happened	Would happen
You	happen	happened	Will happen	Have happened	Would happen
They	happen	happened	Will happen	Have happened	Would happen
It	happens	happened	Will happen	Has happened	Would happen

Pedir: To Ask

	Presente	Pasado	Futuro	Participio	Condicional
I	ask	asked	Will ask	Have asked	Would ask
You	ask	asked	Will ask	Have asked	Would ask
He	asks	asked	Will ask	Has asked	Would ask
She	asks	asked	Will ask	Has asked	Would ask
We	ask	asked	Will ask	Have asked	Would ask
You	ask	asked	Will ask	Have asked	Would ask
They	ask	asked	Will ask	Have asked	Would ask
It	asks	asked	Will ask	Has asked	Would ask

El método de aprendizaje South Beach para inglés conversacional

Verbos esenciales en el idioma inglés

Pedir prestado: To Borrow

	Presente	**Pasado**	**Futuro**	**Participio**	**Condicional**
I	borrow	borrowed	Will borrow	Have borrowed	Would borrow
You	borrow	borrowed	Will borrow	Have borrowed	Would borrow
He	borrows	borrowed	Will borrow	Has borrowed	Would borrow
She	borrows	borrowed	Will borrow	Has borrowed	Would borrow
We	borrow	borrowed	Will borrow	Have borrowed	Would borrow
You	borrow	borrowed	Will borrow	Have borrowed	Would borrow
They	borrow	borrowed	Will borrow	Have borrowed	Would borrow
It	borrows	borrowed	Will borrow	Has borrowed	Would borrow

Pensar: To Think

	Presente	**Pasado**	**Futuro**	**Participio**	**Condicional**
I	think	thought	Will think	Have thought	Would think
You	think	thought	Will think	Have thought	Would think
He	thinks	thought	Will think	Has thought	Would think
She	thinks	thought	Will think	Has thought	Would think
We	think	thought	Will think	Have thought	Would think
You	think	thought	Will think	Have thought	Would think
They	think	thought	Will think	Have thought	Would think
It	thinks	thought	Will think	Has thought	Would think

Perder: To Lose

	Presente	**Pasado**	**Futuro**	**Participio**	**Condicional**
I	lose	lost	Will lose	Have lost	Would lose
You	lose	lost	Will lose	Have lost	Would lose
He	loses	lost	Will lose	Has lost	Would lose
She	loses	lost	Will lose	Has lost	Would lose
We	lose	lost	Will lose	Have lost	Would lose
You	lose	lost	Will lose	Have lost	Would lose
They	lose	lost	Will lose	Have lost	Would lose
It	loses	lost	Will lose	Has lost	Would lose

El método de aprendizaje South Beach para inglés conversacional

Verbos esenciales en el idioma inglés

Perdonar: To pardon

	Presente	Pasado	Futuro	Participio	Condicional
I	pardon	pardoned	Will pardon	Have pardoned	Would pardon
You	pardon	pardoned	Will pardon	Have pardoned	Would pardon
He	pardons	pardoned	Will pardon	Has pardoned	Would pardon
She	pardons	pardoned	Will pardon	Has pardoned	Would pardon
We	pardon	pardoned	Will pardon	Have pardoned	Would pardon
You	pardon	pardoned	Will pardon	Have pardoned	Would pardon
They	pardon	pardoned	Will pardon	Have pardoned	Would pardon
It	pardons	pardoned	Will pardon	Has pardoned	Would pardon

Perdonar: To Forgive

	Presente	Pasado	Futuro	Participio	Condicional
I	forgive	forgave	Will forgive	Have forgiven	Would forgive
You	forgive	forgave	Will forgive	Have forgiven	Would forgive
He	forgives	forgave	Will forgive	Has forgiven	Would forgive
She	forgives	forgave	Will forgive	Has forgiven	Would forgive
We	forgive	forgave	Will forgive	Have forgiven	Would forgive
You	forgive	forgave	Will forgive	Have forgiven	Would forgive
They	forgive	forgave	Will forgive	Have forgiven	Would forgive
It	forgives	forgave	Will forgive	Has forgiven	Would forgive

Permitir: To Allow

	Presente	Pasado	Futuro	Participio	Condicional
I	allow	allowed	Will allow	Have allowed	Would allow
You	allow	allowed	Will allow	Have allowed	Would allow
He	allows	allowed	Will allow	Has allowed	Would allow
She	allows	allowed	Will allow	Has allowed	Would allow
We	allow	allowed	Will allow	Have allowed	Would allow
You	allow	allowed	Will allow	Have allowed	Would allow
They	allow	allowed	Will allow	Have allowed	Would allow
It	allows	allowed	Will allow	Has allowed	Would allow

El método de aprendizaje South Beach para inglés conversacional

Verbos esenciales en el idioma inglés

Poder: Can, May

	Presente	**Pasado**	**Futuro**	**Participio**	**Condicional**
I	Can	Was able to	Will be able to	Have been able to	Could
You	Can	Were able to	Will be able to	Have been able to	Could
He	Can	Was able to	Will be able to	Has been able to	Could
She	Can	Was able to	Will be able to	Has been able to	Could
We	Can	Were able to	Will be able to	Have been able to	Could
You	Can	Were able to	Will be able to	Have been able to	Could
They	Can	Were able to	Will be able to	Have been able to	Could
It	Can	Was able to	Will be able to	Has been able to	Could

Poder: Can, May

	Presente	**Pasado**	**Futuro**	**Participio**	**Condicional**
I	May				
You	May				
He	May				
She	May				
We	May				
You	May				
They	May				
It	May				

Podria; Could

	Presente	**Pasado**	**Futuro**	**Participio**	**Condicional**
I					Could
You					Could
He					Could
She					Could
We					Could
You					Could
They					Could
It					Could

El método de aprendizaje South Beach para inglés conversacional

Verbos esenciales en el idioma inglés

Preguntar: To Ask

	Presente	Pasado	Futuro	Participio	Condicional
I	ask	asked	Will ask	Have asked	Would ask
You	ask	asked	Will ask	Have asked	Would ask
He	asks	asked	Will ask	Has asked	Would ask
She	asks	asked	Will ask	Has asked	Would ask
We	ask	asked	Will ask	Have asked	Would ask
You	ask	asked	Will ask	Have asked	Would ask
They	ask	asked	Will ask	Have asked	Would ask
It	asks	asked	Will ask	Has asked	Would ask

Prestar: To Lend

	Presente	Pasado	Futuro	Participio	Condicional
I	lend	lent	Will lend	Have lent	Would lend
You	lend	lent	Will lend	Have lent	Would lend
He	lends	lent	Will lend	Has lent	Would lend
She	lends	lent	Will lend	Has lent	Would lend
We	lend	lent	Will lend	Have lent	Would lend
You	lend	lent	Will lend	Have lent	Would lend
They	lend	lent	Will lend	Have lent	Would lend
It	lends	lent	Will lend	Has lent	Would lend

Poseer: To Own

	Presente	Pasado	Futuro	Participio	Condicional
I	own	owned	Will own	Have owned	Would own
You	own	owned	Will own	Have owned	Would own
He	owns	owned	Will own	Has owned	Would own
She	owns	owned	Will own	Has owned	Would own
We	own	owned	Will own	Have owned	Would own
You	own	owned	Will own	Have owned	Would own
They	own	owned	Will own	Have owned	Would own
It	owns	owned	Will own	Has owned	Would own

El método de aprendizaje South Beach para inglés conversacional

Verbos esenciales en el idioma inglés

Q Querer: To Want

	Presente	Pasado	Futuro	Participio	Condicional
I	want	wanted	Will want	Have wanted	Would want
You	want	wanted	Will want	Have wanted	Would want
He	wants	wanted	Will want	Has wanted	Would want
She	wants	wanted	Will want	Has wanted	Would want
We	want	wanted	Will want	Have wanted	Would want
You	want	wanted	Will want	Have wanted	Would want
They	want	wanted	Will want	Have wanted	Would want
It	wants	wanted	Will want	Has wanted	Would want

R Rechazar: To Reject

	Presente	Pasado	Futuro	Participio	Condicional
I	reject	rejected	Will reject	Have rejected	Would reject
You	reject	rejected	Will reject	Have rejected	Would reject
He	rejects	rejected	Will reject	Has rejected	Would reject
She	rejects	rejected	Will reject	Has rejected	Would reject
We	reject	rejected	Will reject	Have rejected	Would reject
You	reject	rejected	Will reject	Have rejected	Would reject
They	reject	rejected	Will reject	Have rejected	Would reject
It	rejects	rejected	Will reject	Has rejected	Would reject

Recibir: To Get

	Presente	Pasado	Futuro	Participio	Condicional
I	get	got	Will get	Have gotten	Would get
You	get	got	Will get	Have gotten	Would get
He	gets	got	Will get	Has gotten	Would get
She	gets	got	Will get	Has gotten	Would get
We	get	got	Will get	Have gotten	Would get
You	get	got	Will get	Have gotten	Would get
They	get	got	Will get	Have gotten	Would get
It	gets	got	Will get	Has gotten	Would get

El método de aprendizaje South Beach para inglés conversacional

Verbos esenciales en el idioma inglés

Recordar: To Remember

	Presente	Pasado	Futuro	Participio	Condicional
I	Remember	remembered	Will remember	Have remembered	Would remember
You	Remember	remembered	Will remember	Have remembered	Would remember
He	Remembers	remembered	Will remember	Has remembered	Would remember
She	Remembers	remembered	Will remember	Has remembered	Would remember
We	Remember	remembered	Will remember	Have remembered	Would remember
You	Remember	remembered	Will remember	Have remembered	Would remember
They	Remember	remembered	Will remember	Have remembered	Would remember
It	Remembers	remembered	Will remember	Has remembered	Would remember

Recojer: To Pick

	Presente	Pasado	Futuro	Participio	Condicional
I	pick	picked	Will pick	Have picked	Would pick
You	pick	picked	Will pick	Have picked	Would pick
He	picks	picked	Will pick	Has picked	Would pick
She	picks	picked	Will pick	Has picked	Would pick
We	pick	picked	Will pick	Have picked	Would pick
You	pick	picked	Will pick	Have picked	Would pick
They	pick	picked	Will pick	Have picked	Would pick
It	picks	picked	Will pick	Has picked	Would pick

Regresar: To Return

	Presente	Pasado	Futuro	Participio	Condicional
I	return	returned	Will return	Have returned	Would return
You	return	returned	Will return	Have returned	Would return
He	returns	returned	Will return	Has returned	Would return
She	returns	returned	Will return	Has returned	Would return
We	return	returned	Will return	Have returned	Would return
You	return	returned	Will return	Have returned	Would return
They	return	returned	Will return	Have returned	Would return
It	returns	returned	Will return	Has returned	Would returned

El método de aprendizaje South Beach para inglés conversacional

Verbos esenciales en el idioma inglés

Repetir: To Repeat

	Presente	**Pasado**	**Futuro**	**Participio**	**Condicional**
I	repeat	repeated	Will repeat	Have repeated	Would repeat
You	repeat	repeated	Will repeat	Have repeated	Would repeat
He	repeats	repeated	Will repeat	Has repeated	Would repeat
She	repeats	repeated	Will repeat	Has repeated	Would repeat
We	repeat	repeated	Will repeat	Have repeated	Would repeat
You	repeat	repeated	Will repeat	Have repeated	Would repeat
They	repeat	repeated	Will repeat	Have repeated	Would repeat
It	repeats	repeated	Will repeat	Has repeated	Would repeat

Respetar: To Respect

	Presente	**Pasado**	**Futuro**	**Participio**	**Condicional**
I	respect	respected	Will respect	Have respected	Would respect
You	respect	respected	Will respect	Have respected	Would respect
He	respects	respected	Will respect	Has respected	Would respect
She	respects	respected	Will respect	Has respected	Would respect
We	respect	respected	Will respect	Have respected	Would respect
You	respect	respected	Will respect	Have respected	Would respect
They	respect	respected	Will respect	Have respected	Would respect
It	respects	respected	Will respect	Has respected	Would respect

Responder: To Answer

	Presente	**Pasado**	**Futuro**	**Participio**	**Condicional**
I	answer	answered	Will answer	Have answered	Would answer
You	answer	answered	Will answer	Have answered	Would answer
He	answers	answered	Will answer	Has answered	Would answer
She	answers	answered	Will answer	Has answered	Would answer
We	answer	answered	Will answer	Have answered	Would answer
You	answer	answered	Will answer	Have answered	Would answer
They	answer	answered	Will answer	Have answered	Would answer
It	answers	answered	Will answer	Has answered	Would answer

Verbos esenciales en el idioma inglés

Responder: To Reply

	Presente	Pasado	Futuro	Participio	Condicional
I	reply	replied	Will reply	Have replied	Would reply
You	reply	replied	Will reply	Have replied	Would reply
He	replies	replied	Will reply	Has replied	Would reply
She	replies	replied	Will reply	Has replied	Would reply
We	reply	replied	Will reply	Have replied	Would reply
You	reply	replied	Will reply	Have replied	Would reply
They	reply	replied	Will reply	Have replied	Would reply
It	replies	replied	Will reply	Has replied	Would reply

Reusar: To Refuse

	Presente	Pasado	Futuro	Participio	Condicional
I	refuse	refuseed	Will refuse	Have refuseed	Would refuse
You	refuse	refuseed	Will refuse	Have refuseed	Would refuse
He	refuses	refuseed	Will refuse	Has refuseed	Would refuse
She	refuses	refuseed	Will refuse	Has refuseed	Would refuse
We	refuse	refuseed	Will refuse	Have refuseed	Would refuse
You	refuse	refuseed	Will refuse	Have refuseed	Would refuse
They	refuse	refuseed	Will refuse	Have refuseed	Would refuse
It	refuses	refuseed	Will refuse	Has refuseed	Would respect

Saber: To Know

	Presente	Pasado	Futuro	Participio	Condicional
I	know	knew	Will know	Have known	Would know
You	know	knew	Will know	Have known	Would know
He	knows	knew	Will know	Has known	Would know
She	knows	knew	Will know	Has known	Would know
We	know	knew	Will know	Have known	Would know
You	know	knew	Will know	Have known	Would know
They	know	knew	Will know	Have known	Would know
It	knows	knew	Will know	Has known	Would know

El método de aprendizaje South Beach para inglés conversacional

Verbos esenciales en el idioma inglés

Salir: To Exit

	Presente	**Pasado**	**Futuro**	**Participio**	**Condicional**
I	Exit	Exited	Will Exit	Have Exited	Would Exit
You	Exit	Exited	Will Exit	Have Exited	Would Exit
He	Exits	Exited	Will Exit	Has Exited	Would Exit
She	Exits	Exited	Will Exit	Has Exited	Would Exit
We	Exit	Exited	Will Exit	Have Exited	Would Exit
You	Exit	Exited	Will Exit	Have Exited	Would Exit
They	Exit	Exited	Will Exit	Have Exited	Would Exit
It	Exits	Exited	Will Exit	Has Exited	Would Exit

Salvar: To Save

	Presente	**Pasado**	**Futuro**	**Participio**	**Condicional**
I	Save	Saved	Will Save	Have Saved	Would Save
You	Save	Saved	Will Save	Have Saved	Would Save
He	Saves	Saved	Will Save	Has Saved	Would Save
She	Saves	Saved	Will Save	Has Saved	Would Save
We	Save	Saved	Will Save	Have Saved	Would Save
You	Save	Saved	Will Save	Have Saved	Would Save
They	Save	Saved	Will Save	Have Saved	Would Save
It	Saves	Saved	Will Save	Has Saved	Would Save

Satisfacer: To Satisfy

	Presente	**Pasado**	**Futuro**	**Participio**	**Condicional**
I	Satisfy	Satisfied	Will Satisfy	Have Satisfied	Would Satisfy
You	Satisfy	Satisfied	Will Satisfy	Have Satisfied	Would Satisfy
He	Satisfies	Satisfied	Will Satisfy	Has Satisfied	Would Satisfy
She	Satisfies	Satisfied	Will Satisfy	Has Satisfied	Would Satisfy
We	Satisfy	Satisfied	Will Satisfy	Have Satisfied	Would Satisfy
You	Satisfy	Satisfied	Will Satisfy	Have Satisfied	Would Satisfy
They	Satisfy	Satisfied	Will Satisfy	Have Satisfied	Would Satisfy
It	Satisfies	Satisfied	Will Satisfy	Has Satisfied	Would Satisfy

El método de aprendizaje South Beach para inglés conversacional

Verbos esenciales en el idioma inglés

Seguir: To Follow

	Presente	Pasado	Futuro	Participio	Condicional
I	follow	followed	WIll follow	Have followed	Would follow
You	follow	followed	Will follow	Have followed	Would follow
He	follows	followed	Will follow	Has followed	Would follow
She	follows	followed	Will follow	Has followed	Would follow
We	follow	followed	Will follow	Have followed	Would follow
You	follow	followed	Will follow	Have followed	Would follow
They	follow	followed	Will follow	Have followed	Would follow
It	follows	followed	Will follow	Has followed	Would follow

Sentir: To Feel

	Presente	Pasado	Futuro	Participio	Condicional
I	feel	felt	Will feel	Have felt	Would feel
You	feel	felt	Will feel	Have felt	Would feel
He	feels	felt	Will feel	Has felt	Would feel
She	feels	felt	Will feel	Has felt	Would feel
We	feel	felt	Will feel	Have felt	Would feel
You	feel	felt	Will feel	Have felt	Would feel
They	feel	felt	Will feel	Have felt	Would feel
It	feels	felt	Will feel	Has felt	Would feel

Ser: To Be

	Presente	Pasado	Futuro	Participio	Condicional
I	Am	was	Will be	Have been	Would be
You	Are	were	Will be	Have been	Would be
He	Is	was	Will be	Has been	Would be
She	Is	was	Will be	Has been	Would be
We	Are	were	Will be	Have been	Would be
You	Are	were	Will be	Have been	Would be
They	Are	were	Will be	Have been	Would be
It	Is	was	Will be	Has been	Would be

El método de aprendizaje South Beach para inglés conversacional

Verbos esenciales en el idioma inglés

Solicitar: To Request

	Presente	Pasado	Futuro	Participio	Condicional
I	request	requested	Will request	Have requested	Would request
You	request	requested	Will request	Have requested	Would request
He	requests	requested	Will request	Has requested	Would request
She	requests	requested	Will request	Has requested	Would request
We	request	requested	Will request	Have requested	Would request
You	request	requested	Will request	Have requested	Would request
They	request	requested	Will request	Have requested	Would request
It	requests	requested	Will request	Has requested	Would request

Solucionar: To Solve

	Presente	Pasado	Futuro	Participio	Condicional
I	solve	solved	Will solve	Have solved	Would solve
You	solve	solved	Will solve	Have solved	Would solve
He	solves	solved	Will solve	Has solved	Would solve
She	solves	solved	Will solve	Has solved	Would solve
We	solve	solved	Will solve	Have solved	Would solve
You	solve	solved	Will solve	Have solved	Would solve
They	solve	solved	Will solve	Have solved	Would solve
It	solves	solved	Will solve	Has solved	Would solve

Sonreir: To Smile

	Presente	Pasado	Futuro	Participio	Condicional
I	smile	smiled	Will smile	Have smiled	Would smile
You	smile	smiled	Will smile	Have smiled	Would smile
He	smiles	smiled	Will smile	Has smiled	Would smile
She	smiles	smiled	Will smile	Has smiled	Would smile
We	smile	smiled	Will smile	Have smiled	Would smile
You	smile	smiled	Will smile	Have smiled	Would smile
They	smile	smiled	Will smile	Have smiled	Would smile
It	smiles	smiled	Will smile	Has smiled	Would smile

El método de aprendizaje South Beach para inglés conversacional

Verbos esenciales en el idioma inglés

T   Temer: To Fear

	Presente	Pasado	Futuro	Participio	Condicional
I	fear	feared	Will fear	Have feared	Would fear
You	fear	feared	Will fear	Have feared	Would fear
He	fears	feared	Will fear	Has feared	Would fear
She	fears	feared	Will fear	Has feared	Would fear
We	fear	feared	Will fear	Have feared	Would fear
You	fear	feared	Will fear	Have feared	Would fear
They	fear	feared	Will fear	Have feared	Would fear
It	fears	feared	Will fear	Has feared	Would fear

Tener: To Have

	Presente	Pasado	Futuro	Participio	Condicional
I	have	had	Will have	Have had	Would have
You	have	had	Will have	Have had	Would have
He	has	had	Will have	Has had	Would have
She	has	had	Will have	Has had	Would have
We	have	had	Will have	Have had	Would have
You	have	had	Will have	Have had	Would have
They	have	had	Will have	Have had	Would have
It	has	had	Will have	Has had	Would have

Terminar: To Finish

	Presente	Pasado	Futuro	Participio	Condicional
I	finish	finished	Will finish	Have finished	Would finish
You	finish	finished	Will finish	Have finished	Would finish
He	finishs	finished	Will finish	Has finished	Would finish
She	finishs	finished	Will finish	Has finished	Would finish
We	finish	finished	Will finish	Have finished	Would finish
You	finish	finished	Will finish	Have finished	Would finish
They	finish	finished	Will finish	Have finished	Would finish
It	finishs	finished	Will finish	Has finished	Would finish

El método de aprendizaje South Beach para inglés conversacional

Verbos esenciales en el idioma inglés

Trabajar: To Work

	Presente	Pasado	Futuro	Participio	Condicional
I	work	worked	Will work	Have worked	Would work
You	work	worked	Will work	Have worked	Would work
He	works	worked	Will work	Has worked	Would work
She	works	worked	Will work	Has worked	Would work
We	work	worked	Will work	Have worked	Would work
You	work	worked	Will work	Have worked	Would work
They	work	worked	Will work	Have worked	Would work
It	works	worked	Will work	Has worked	Would work

Traer: To Bring

	Presente	Pasado	Futuro	Participio	Condicional
I	bring	brought	Will bring	Have brought	Would bring
You	bring	brought	Will bring	Have brought	Would bring
He	brings	brought	Will bring	Has brought	Would bring
She	brings	brought	Will bring	Has brought	Would bring
We	bring	brought	Will bring	Have brought	Would bring
You	bring	brought	Will bring	Have brought	Would bring
They	bring	brought	Will bring	Have brought	Would bring
It	brings	brought	Will bring	Has brought	Would bring

Tomar: To Take

	Presente	Pasado	Futuro	Participio	Condicional
I	take	took	Will take	Have taken	Would take
You	take	took	Will take	Have taken	Would take
He	takes	took	Will take	Has taken	Would take
She	takes	took	Will take	Has taken	Would take
We	take	took	Will take	Have taken	Would take
You	take	took	Will take	Have taken	Would take
They	take	took	Will take	Have taken	Would take
It	takes	took	Will take	Has taken	Would take

El método de aprendizaje South Beach para inglés conversacional

Verbos esenciales en el idioma inglés

Tratar: To Try

	Presente	Pasado	Futuro	Participio	Condicional
I	try	tried	Will try	Have tried	Would try
You	try	tried	Will try	Have tried	Would try
He	tries	tried	Will try	Has tried	Would try
She	tries	tried	Will try	Has tried	Would try
We	try	tried	Will try	Have tried	Would try
You	try	tried	Will try	Have tried	Would try
They	try	tried	Will try	Have tried	Would try
It	tries	tried	Will try	Has tried	Would try

Tocar: To Play (Instrumento)

	Presente	Pasado	Futuro	Participio	Condicional
I	play	played	Will play	Have played	Would play
You	play	played	Will play	Have played	Would play
He	plays	played	Will play	Has played	Would play
She	plays	played	Will play	Has played	Would play
We	play	played	Will play	Have played	Would play
You	play	played	Will play	Have played	Would play
They	play	played	Will play	Have played	Would play
It	plays	played	Will play	Has played	Would play

Usar: To Use, To Wear

	Presente	Pasado	Futuro	Participio	Condicional
I	use	used	Will use	Have used	Would use
You	use	used	Will use	Have used	Would use
He	uses	used	Will use	Has used	Would use
She	uses	used	Will use	Has used	Would use
We	use	used	Will use	Have used	Would use
You	use	used	Will use	Have used	Would use
They	use	used	Will use	Have used	Would use
It	uses	used	Will use	Has used	Would use

El método de aprendizaje South Beach para inglés conversacional

Verbos esenciales en el idioma inglés

Utilizar: To Utilize

	Presente	**Pasado**	**Futuro**	**Participio**	**Condicional**
I	utilize	utilized	Will utilize	Have utilized	Would utilize
You	utilize	utilized	Will utilize	Have utilized	Would utilize
He	utilizes	utilized	Will utilize	Has utilized	Would utilize
She	utilizes	utilized	Will utilize	Has utilized	Would utilize
We	utilize	utilized	Will utilize	Have utilized	Would utilize
You	utilize	utilized	Will utilize	Have utilized	Would utilize
They	utilize	utilized	Will utilize	Have utilized	Would utilize
It	utilizes	utilized	Will utilize	Has utilized	Would utilize

Valorar: To Value

	Presente	**Pasado**	**Futuro**	**Participio**	**Condicional**
I	value	valued	Will value	Have valued	Would value
You	value	valued	Will value	Have valued	Would value
He	values	valued	Will value	Has valued	Would value
She	values	valued	Will value	Has valued	Would value
We	value	valued	Will value	Have valued	Would value
You	value	valued	Will value	Have valued	Would value
They	value	valued	Will value	Have valued	Would value
It	values	valued	Will value	Has valued	Would value

Vender: To Sell

	Presente	**Pasado**	**Futuro**	**Participio**	**Condicional**
I	sell	sold	Will sell	Have sold	Would sell
You	sell	sold	Will sell	Have sold	Would sell
He	sells	sold	Will sell	Has sold	Would sell
She	sells	sold	Will sell	Has sold	Would sell
We	sell	sold	Will sell	Have sold	Would sell
You	sell	sold	Will sell	Have sold	Would sell
They	sell	sold	Will sell	Have sold	Would sell
It	sells	sold	Will sell	Has sold	Would sell

El método de aprendizaje South Beach para inglés conversacional

Verbos esenciales en el idioma inglés

Venir: To Come

	Presente	Pasado	Futuro	Participio	Condicional
I	come	came	Will come	Have come	Would come
You	come	came	Will come	Have come	Would come
He	comes	came	Will come	Has come	Would come
She	comes	came	Will come	Has come	Would come
We	come	came	Will come	Have come	Would come
You	come	came	Will come	Have come	Would come
They	come	came	Will come	Have come	Would come
It	comes	came	Will come	Has come	Would come

Ver: To See

	Presente	Pasado	Futuro	Participio	Condicional
I	see	saw	Will see	Have seen	Would see
You	see	saw	Will see	Have seen	Would see
He	sees	saw	Will see	Has seen	Would see
She	sees	saw	Will see	Has seen	Would see
We	see	saw	Will see	Have seen	Would see
You	see	saw	Will see	Have seen	Would see
They	see	saw	Will see	Have seen	Would see
It	sees	saw	Will see	Has seen	Would see

Vestir: To Dress

	Presente	Pasado	Futuro	Participio	Condicional
I	dress	dressed	Will dress	Have dressed	Would dress
You	dress	dressed	Will dress	Have dressed	Would dress
He	dresses	dressed	Will dress	Has dressed	Would dress
She	dresses	dressed	Will dress	Has dressed	Would dress
We	dress	dressed	Will dress	Have dressed	Would dress
You	dress	dressed	Will dress	Have dressed	Would dress
They	dress	dressed	Will dress	Have dressed	Would dress
It	dresses	dressed	Will dress	Has dressed	Would dress

El método de aprendizaje South Beach para inglés conversacional

Verbos esenciales en el idioma inglés

Viajar: To Travel

	Presente	Pasado	Futuro	Participio	Condicional
I	travel	traveled	Will travel	Have traveled	Would travel
You	travel	traveled	Will travel	Have traveled	Would travel
He	travels	traveled	Will travel	Has traveled	Would travel
She	travels	traveled	Will travel	Has traveled	Would travel
We	travel	traveled	Will travel	Have traveled	Would travel
You	travel	traveled	Will travel	Have traveled	Would travel
They	travel	traveled	Will travel	Have traveled	Would travel
It	travels	traveled	Will travel	Has traveled	Would travel

Visitar: To Visit

	Presente	Pasado	Futuro	Participio	Condicional
I	visit	visited	Will visit	Have visited	Would visit
You	visit	visited	Will visit	Have visited	Would visit
He	visits	visited	Will visit	Has visited	Would visit
She	visits	visited	Will visit	Has visited	Would visit
We	visit	visited	Will visit	Have visited	Would visit
You	visit	visited	Will visit	Have visited	Would visit
They	visit	visited	Will visit	Have visited	Would visit
It	visits	visited	Will visit	Has visited	Would visit

Vivir: To Live

	Presente	Pasado	Futuro	Participio	Condicional
I	live	lived	Will live	Have lived	Would live
You	live	lived	Will live	Have lived	Would live
He	lives	lived	Will live	Has lived	Would live
She	lives	lived	Will live	Has lived	Would live
We	live	lived	Will live	Have lived	Would live
You	live	lived	Will live	Have lived	Would live
They	live	lived	Will live	Have lived	Would live
It	lives	lived	Will live	Has lived	Would smile

El método de aprendizaje South Beach para inglés conversacional

Notas

1-**Gerundio / (Gerund):** Los verbos en gerundio en Inglés terminan en "ing" y en español en "endo, iendo, o ando". Además requieren que el verbo "To Be"(Ser o Estar) les preceda. Para practicar frases en inglés en gerundio simplemente coloque el verbo "To Be" (Ser o Estar) de acuerdo a la conjugación antes del verbo en inglés terminado en "ing".

(I - Am) – Yo – Estoy
(You – Are) – Usted – Está
(He – is) – El – Está
(She – is) Ella – Está
(We – Are) – Nosotros – Estamos
(You – Are) – Ustedes – Están
(They – Are) – Ellos – Están
(It – is) – Eso/Esto – Está

Ejemplos:

Yo estoy escribiendo – I Am Writing
Usted está esperando – You Are Waiting
El está llamando – He is Calling
Ella está cocinando – She Is Cooking
Nosotros estamos cocinando – We Are Eating
Ustedes están comiendo – You Are Eating
Ellos están viniendo – They Are Coming

El método de aprendizaje South Beach para inglés conversacional

Notas

2- **Pasado Participio / (Past Participle):** Los verbos en Pasado Participio en español en "ido o ado". Además requieren que el verbo "To Have"(Haber) les preceda.

Para practicar frases en inglés en Pasado Participio simplemente coloque el verbo "To Have" (Haber) de acuerdo a la conjugación antes del verbo en Participio.

(I - Am) – Yo – He
(You – Are) – Usted – Ha
(He – is) – El – Ha
(She – is) Ella – Ha
(We – Are) – Nosotros – Hemos
(You – Are) – Ustedes – Han
(They – Are) – Ellos – Han
(It – is) – Eso/Esto – Ha

Ejemplos:

Yo he esperado – I Have Waited

Usted ha recibido correo – You Have Gotten Mail

Ella ha dormido bien - She Has Slept Well

El ha comido tarde – He Has Eaten Late

Nosotros hemos corrido en la manaña – We Have Run in the Morning

Ustedes han ido a clases temprano – You Have Gone to class early

Ellos han hecho la tarea juntos – They Have Done the Homework Together